D1025760

Disclaimer

All material on Peapil.com and this book is provided for your information only and may not be construed as medical advice or instruction. No action or inaction should be taken based solely on the contents of this information; instead, readers should consult appropriate health professionals on any matter relating to their health and well-being. If you think you may have a medical emergency, call your doctor or 911 immediately.

The content of this book (text, graphics and images) is not intended to be a substitute for professional medical advice, diagnosis, or treatment. Always seek the advice of your physician or other qualified health provider with any questions you may have regarding a medical condition.

Never disregard professional medical advice or delay in seeking it because of something you have read in this book. The information and opinions expressed here are believed to be accurate, based on the best judgment available to the authors. Readers who fail to consult with appropriate health authorities assume the risk of any injuries. Reliance on any information and content provided by Peapil Publishing and this book is solely at your own risk.

The publisher is not responsible for errors or omissions.

Rev 1.1

TABLE OF CONTENTS

INTRODUCTION

Mediterranean food has long been recognized as some of the healthiest and most nutritious out there. Lowering the chances of heart and cognitive problems and thus boosting longevity, the diet's benefits are documented and acknowledged worldwide. The groups of people living along the Mediterranean Sea are among the healthiest people in the world, and for good reason: the food they eat.

While everyone wants to be more cautious about the food they put into their bodies, eating healthy is often expensive. Fresh foods are frequently marked up in price due to their availability (or lack thereof), making preservatives much more appealing for the budget. Most people don't have the yard space to grow fresh produce, or simply live in regions unsuitable for the desired fruits and vegetables. Marketers understand all of these problems and use them against consumers.

Ever notice how the foods that are the worst for our bodies have the catchiest names and fanciest packaging?

If you're reading this, chances are you've read our first book, *The Mediterranean Refresh*, and maybe even its add-on, *The Mediterranean Refresh: Meal Plan*. Both books lay a great groundwork for entering the Mediterranean diet and cuisine, but feature recipes that run a touch expensive for people on more modest budgets.

The Mediterranean Refresh: Meals on a Budget is a companion to the first two editions for folks who want to monitor both their nutrition and their pockets. Let's face it: eating healthy isn't always easy on the wallet, but it doesn't have to break the bank either. This third book in the series introduces 60 brand-new recipes not seen in the previous two editions. Each recipe is budget-friendly (hovering around $3 per serving), while still maintaining the extreme health benefits of Mediterranean cuisine.

But what are these supposedly life-changing health benefits that we've been rambling on about?

Studies have shown that healthy fats such as extra-virgin olive oil and nuts drastically decrease the risks of breast cancer, diabetes and cognitive diseases. Lowering the intake of red meats, processed foods and refined grains can help prevent heart disease and strokes, especially when following the Mediterranean lifestyle.

Fish and seafood play a large role in the diet's health benefits as well. The Omega-3 acids found in a wide array of fish can help maintain brain and heart health, while other foods found under the sea provide similar perks.

There have also been reports published that link the Mediterranean diet to lowered depression rates. When compared with the "American diet" (processed foods, fast food, etc.), studies have stated that the diet has a 33% reduced risk of depression.

Simply put, Mediterranean cuisine not only tastes good but reduces the risk of many frightening diseases.

Given the tremendous physical and mental health benefits, it's almost a no-brainer to give the Mediterranean Diet a try and see all the amazing benefits for yourself! Not only that, but the food will also take your taste buds on a flavor trip, AND your piggy bank will remain intact. As previously mentioned, each recipe costs roughly $3 per serving. To put this into perspective, the average commercially-prepared dish is approximately $13 per person. Even your favorite value meal from McDonald's costs $5.

Maybe you don't eat out much, and instead cook at home for both the financial and health benefits. The average home-cooked meal costs $4-$5 in groceries per person. Not only do these 60 recipes save you large sums of money compared to eating out, but they can save more than $300 a year (per person) compared to other home cooking.

The great thing about Mediterranean food is that there's a little something for everyone. No two people have exactly the same tastes and preferences, but with its wide array of flavors and ingredients, anyone can find their place in this cuisine.

Whether you're trying to eat healthier, or just simply save a few pennies, *The Mediterranean Refresh: Meals on a Budget* is worth a shot. The health benefits of the cuisine are endless, and unless you solely consume instant ramen, you can't get much cheaper than the 60 recipes in this book.

So what are you waiting for? Hop on the Mediterranean lifestyle and start bettering yourself and your wallet right now!

Yummy Mediterranean Recipes on a Budget

GRAIN SALAD
with Summer Vegetables

This awesome and delicious grain salad is the perfect lunch to prepare in advance for any season. However, this one, filled with protein-rich quinoa and seasonal summer vegetables, is particularly tasty for the last few weeks of summer. It's easy enough to eat on the hottest days of August, and it always fills you up. The best part? Add a ridiculously quick topping that starts with a cup of your favorite pesto.

INGREDIENTS

For salad

1 ½	Cup	Quinoa, rinse well
2 ¾	Cup	Water
1	Tsp.	Kosher salt
1	Pint	Cherry tomatoes (about 2 cups), halved
1		Large English cucumber, chopped
3		Small peppers, seeded and chopped
		Kosher salt, to taste
		Freshly ground black pepper

For topping

1	Cup	Homemade or prepared basil pesto
1.5	Tbsp.	Red wine vinegar

INSTRUCTIONS

Cook quinoa:

1. Mix the quinoa, water and tablespoon of salt in a medium bowl and bring to a boil. Reduce heat, cover, and simmer until quinoa is soft and all of the liquid is absorbed (about 15 minutes). Stir with a fork, place the quinoa on a baking sheet with edges, spread evenly, and put in the fridge for 10 to 15 minutes until it has cooled completely.

Make a vinaigrette:

2. Put the pesto and vinegar in a large bowl and mix.

Collect salad:

3. Add the cooled quinoa, cucumbers, peppers, and tomatoes to the dressing. Stir and distribute evenly. Taste and season with salt and pepper. Best served at room temperature or chilled.

Nutrition

Calories:	252	**Carbohydrates:** 27.8 g		**Protein:**	7.1 g
Fat:	12.8 g	**Fiber:**	4.1 g		

GARLIC BASIL
Sausage Farrotto

T he result is a whole grain version of one of my favorite dishes, made with farro instead of traditional rice, and used as a round meal with added sausage. Each bite is usually creamy and crispy thanks to the fresh juice of garlic, basil and lemon.

INGREDIENTS

2	Cups	Farro
2	Tbsp.	Olive oil
⅓		Small onion, cut into cubes
4		Chopped cloves of garlic
		Kosher salt
		Freshly ground black pepper
½	Cup	Dry white wine
4	Cups	Chicken broth with low sodium content, heated over low heat
1 ½	Pounds	Your choice of sausage
1	Cup	Lightly chopped fresh basil leaves
3	Tbsp.	Unsalted butter
2	Tbsp.	Freshly squeezed lemon juice

INSTRUCTIONS

1. Place the farro in a large bowl and cover with 2 inches of water. Bring to a boil, reduce heat and simmer until the farro softens for 20 to 30 minutes but bites firmly. Then drain.

2. Heat the oil over medium heat until it shimmers, using the same pan. Add the onions and cook for 3 to 5 minutes until they are soft. Add the garlic and cook for another minute. Stir in the farro with a pinch of salt and a generous amount of ground pepper.

3. Add the wine and deglaze the bottom of the bowl. Stir with wooden spoon for 1 minute until everything has evaporated.

4. Add the lukewarm broth and simmer until the farro has absorbed almost all of the broth. Continue adding the broth and stir until it's incorporated and until the farro is creamy, a total of 8 to 10 minutes. At this point, you should have at least half a cup of hot soup.

5. Season the sausage with salt and pepper and add to the pan. Keep stirring until the sausage becomes caramelized on both sides, about 2 to 3 minutes. If needed, add more broth to your desired texture and taste. Remove from the heat and stir in the basil, butter and lemon juice. Season to taste with salt and pepper. Serve immediately.

Nutrition

Calories:	415	**Carbohydrates:**	46.2 g	**Protein:**	27.2 g
Fat:	13.7 g	**Fiber:**	6.7 g		

SPRING SALAD
with Asparagus and Meyer Lemon

This salad is a bit of a celebration of the fact that the Meyer lemon season overlaps with the commencement of the spring asparagus festival. Sweet citrus fruits go well with a chewy mixture of farro, pearl couscous and crispy asparagus. Add a few almonds and goat cheese and lunch is ready!

Serves: 6 to 8

INGREDIENTS

8	Oz.	Pearled (1 ¼ cup) farro
1 ¼	Cup	Pearl (Israeli) couscous or Trader Joe's Harvest Grains Blend
2		Meyer lemons, squeezed and juiced
1	kg.	Asparagus, cut
1	Tbsp.	Olive oil
1	Cup	Sliced almonds or walnuts, toasted
4	Oz.	Soft goat cheese, chilled and puréed
1	Tbsp.	Walnut oil, if desired
		Salt and freshly ground black pepper to taste

INSTRUCTIONS

1. In a 2-quart pan, boil 3 cups of water. Salt generously and add farro, cover and cook for 15 minutes or al dente. (If you are substituting another grain such as spelt or wheat berries, follow the instructions on the package.)
2. In the meantime, cook the pearl couscous or grain mixture in another pan, according to the instructions on the package.
3. Place the pearl couscous on a large baking sheet and allow to cool. Squeeze the lemon over the grains and stir.
4. Remove the woody ends of the asparagus and cut into 1-inch pieces. In a large saucepan, heat 1 teaspoon of olive oil over medium heat and barely cook the asparagus until crispy – about 2 minutes.
5. Place the chilled asparagus stalks in a large bowl. Add sliced almonds and goat cheese.
6. Mix together Meyer lemon juice with ¼ cup of olive and walnut oil. Season the salad and add salt and pepper to taste.

Nutrition

Calories:	388	Carbohydrates:	48.2 g	Protein:	14.3 g
Fat:	17.0 g	Fiber:	7.6 g		

WARM FARRO SALAD

with Roasted Vegetables

and Fontina

This recipe is inspired by a similar salad at Caffe Falai, a small, sleek restaurant in downtown Soho New York. When we ate it, we knew it was an excellent healthy dish that was perfect for lunch or dinner. We couldn't believe how simple (and honestly better) our home version was. Oh, and those grape tomatoes? They are grown in Connecticut.

INGREDIENTS

2		Medium carrots, peeled and cut into small pieces
1	Cup	Grape tomatoes
8		Cremini mushrooms, cut into small pieces
3	Cloves	Garlic, peeled and cut into quarters
1		Small red onion, sliced
4	Tbsp.	Olive oil
1	Tsp.	Kosher salt
½	Tsp.	Pepper
½	Small cup	Chicory, pierced and cut into pieces
1	Cup	Farro
3	Oz.	Fontina cheese, cut into small cubes
		A small handful of chopped parsley
1	Tbsp.	Balsamic vinegar

INSTRUCTIONS

1. Preheat oven to 400° F.
2. Mix carrots, tomatoes, mushrooms, garlic and onions in a large bowl. Add 2 table-spoons of olive oil, salt and pepper and stir. Spread the vegetables on a baking sheet lined with foil and bake for 15 minutes, stirring. Spread the radicchio over the tray and stir. Cover with a little oil and cook for another 10 minutes.
3. Meanwhile, rinse and drain the farro. Bring 2 cups of water to a boil, season with salt and add the farro. Cook for 12–15 minutes, until soft but still firm in the middle. Then drain.
4. Mix the cooked farro and vegetables, then add the fontina and parsley. Coat the remaining vegetables with olive oil and balsamic vinegar, season with salt and pepper and sprinkle onto farro mixture.

Nutrition

Calories:	506	**Carbohydrates:** 54.1 g		**Protein:**	17.0 g
Fat:	27.1 g	**Fiber:**	9.1 g		

GRAIN SALAD
with Tomato, Corn and Basil

This simple cereal (grain) salad is one meal we always had ready to go: we had cooked wheat berries on hand; I brought fresh tomatoes and corn from the market; and for dinner, folded in basil, goat cheese, and a thick lemon topping. The result? Our new summertime salad.

INGREDIENTS

For salad:

1	Cup	Wheat berries
1	Tbsp.	Extra-virgin olive oil
1		Large finely chopped shallot *(approximately ⅓ cup)*
2	Ears	Fresh corn, peeled, sliced *(approximately 1¾ cup)*
3	Chopped cloves	Garlic
1 ½	Cups	Cherry tomatoes, quarters
¾	Cup	Chopped fresh basil
½	Cup	Feta or goat cheese

For topping:

1	Tbsp.	Fresh lemon zest
2	Tbsp.	Fresh lemon juice
2	Tbsp.	Extra-virgin olive oil
½	Tsp.	Dijon mustard
1	Tsp.	Kosher salt
½	Tsp.	Fresh black pepper

INSTRUCTIONS

1. Mix the wheat berries, 3 cups cold water, and ¼ teaspoon salt in a medium-sized pan and boil. Reduce heat, cover and simmer for 30 minutes to 1 hour or until wheat berries are cooked and have absorbed most of the liquid (see cooking instructions below). Remove from the heat and let stand for ten minutes. Drain excess water.

2. In a large saucepan with a non-stick coating, heat the olive oil and add the shallots. Cook for 3 to 4 minutes on medium heat. Add the corn and increase the heat to medium-high. Cook the corn until it browns along the edges and soften for about 10 minutes. Add the garlic and stir to combine. Let it cook for another 2 to 3 minutes.

3. To prepare the topping, stir in the lemon zest, lemon juice, olive oil, mustard, salt and pepper until smooth.

4. Place the cooked wheat berries, corn mixture, tomato and basil along with the dressing in a bowl. Season with salt and pepper. Fold in the goat cheese and serve at room temperature (it's also nice when served cold). Cover the remnants of the berries and cool them for up to 3 days.

Nutrition

Calories:	248	**Carbohydrates:** 33.2 g		**Protein:**	7.9 g
Fat:	11.1 g	**Fiber:**	5.4 g		

FRIED EGGPLANT

With Brown Rice and Turmeric Tahini

This bowl is perfect as a meal during the week because it is infinitely customizable. Consider the formula it is based on (vegetables + legumes + grains + tahini sauce) as a wonderful foundation for building your own soothing bowl of goodness.

INGREDIENTS

For eggplant and bowl:

3	Medium-sized	Eggplants (about 2 pounds in total), cut into ½-inch circles
3	Tbsp.	Olive oil
1	Tbsp.	Za'atara
		Kosher salt
		Freshly ground black pepper
4	Cups	Cooked brown rice, warm or at room temperature
1	(14-oz.) Can	Salted beans, drained and washed
¾	Cup	Mushrooms, sliced
⅓	Cup	Coarsely chopped fresh mint leaves
½	Cup	Red pepper

For turmeric tahini:

½	Cup	Tahini
⅓	Cup	Water
1	Tbsp.	Olive oil
2	Tsp.	Maple syrup
1	Tsp.	Freshly squeezed lemon juice
½	Tsp.	Ground turmeric
1	Small clove	Garlic, chopped
		Kosher salt

INSTRUCTIONS

Baked eggplant:

1. Place the rack in the middle of the oven and preheat to 400° F.
2. Place the eggplant on a baking sheet. Season with oil and sprinkle with Za'atar and salt.
3. Bake for 15 minutes. Turn the eggplant and cook for another 10 minutes. Remove from the oven and season with more salt and black pepper. Put aside.

Make Tahini:

1. Put tahini and water in a small bowl and beat until smooth and thick. Stir in remaining ingredients and season with salt.
2. Divide the rice into 4 bowls. Finish with chickpeas and eggplant. Sprinkle with coriander, mint and pomegranate seeds. Sprinkle turmeric tahini generously over it.

Nutrition

Calories:	795	Carbohydrates:	107.3 g	Protein:	279.7 g
Fat:	35.1 g	Fiber:	27.0 g		

QUINOA
Tabbouleh

Quinoa is one of my favorite grains: breakfast, lunch or dinner. I am a convinced fanatic. It has a roasted flavor and a slightly chewy texture that makes it excellent alone or in a salad like this. (PS: Add scrambled eggs and it's a very satisfying meal!)

INGREDIENTS

1	Cup	Red quinoa
½		Medium red onion, chopped
2		Medium tomatoes, chopped
2	Cups	Chopped parsley (1 large bunch)
½	Cup	Mint (1 small bunch)
2	Cloves	Garlic, minced
¼	Cup	Extra-virgin olive oil
2	Tbsp.	Lemon juice, plus extra to taste
		Salt and pepper
1 ¼	Cup	Feta cheese, optional

INSTRUCTIONS

1. Rinse the quinoa in cold water, then mix with 2 cups of water and ½ teaspoon of salt in a medium skillet. Bring to a boil, then reduce the heat to medium-low, cover and cook until the quinoa is tender and soft, about 20 minutes.

2. In the meantime, dip the onions in a bowl of cold water. This softens the bite and makes it more pleasant to eat when raw.

3. Pour the cooked quinoa into a large bowl and allow it to cool almost to room temperature. Quinoa should be slightly warm to the touch. You can speed up this process by spreading the quinoa thinly and stirring occasionally.

4. Drain the red onion. Add the onion, tomato, parsley, mint, and garlic to the hot quinoa. Beat the olive oil and lemon juice with ½ teaspoon of salt. Pour this over the salad and stir to combine. If you use it, chop the feta cheese on the salad and stir. Try a tablespoon of salad and add more salt or pepper to taste.

5. Serve at room temperature or cold. This salad is even better the next day, after the fusion of flavors.

Nutrition

Calories:	125	**Carbohydrates:**	14.2 g	**Protein:**	3.1 g
Fat:	6.6 g	**Fiber:**	2.2 g		

HOT BULGUR AND LENTIL SALAD
with Grilled Shrimp

I have found it best to put the shrimp pan into the oven to cook while the bulgur cooks. This technique of roasting, where you get all the flavor of the shrimp because it doesn't cook in water, is so simple that is one of the reasons why I always try to have a bag of shrimp in my freezer (I thaw the shrimp before grilling them). Although I like this warm salad, leftovers make an excellent lunch for work the next day.

INGREDIENTS

3	Tbsp.	Olive oil, divided
½		Medium onion, finely chopped
1	Tsp.	Salt, plus more to taste
		Freshly ground black pepper
1	Cup	Dried green, brown or french lentils
1	Cup	Chicken or vegetable broth
1	Cup	Water
1	Cup	Amoroso tomatoes
½	Cup	Bulgur
1	Tbsp.	Red wine vinegar, and more if necessary
2	Pounds	Large shrimp, uncooked, peeled and minced
⅓	Cup	Fresh Italian parsley, finely chopped

INSTRUCTIONS

1. Place the rack in the middle of the oven and preheat to 400° F.

2. In a medium saucepan, heat 2 tablespoons of oil over medium heat. Add the onion and ¼ teaspoon salt, season with pepper and cook, stirring occasionally, until the onion softens, about 8 minutes.

3. To the onion and oil, add the lentils and stir. Add the broth and water and bring to a boil, then reduce the heat to low and simmer until the lentils are tender, 20 to 30 minutes. Meanwhile, cut the red peppers into small cubes.

4. When the lentils are ready, remove them from the heat and add the peppers and bulgur. Cover and set aside until the bulgur softens, about 10 minutes. Meanwhile, grill the shrimp.

5. Place the shrimp on a baking sheet, cover with the tablespoon of remaining oil, season with salt and pepper. Arrange in a straight line and cook until cloudy and cooked throughout, 6 to 8 minutes.

6. Drain any excess liquid from the bulgur and lentils. Add the vinegar and parsley; taste; and add salt, pepper, and more vinegar as needed. Transfer to serving bowls and garnish with grilled shrimp and tomatoes.

Nutrition

Calories:	414	**Carbohydrates:**	48.2 g	**Protein:**	30.0 g
Fat:	12.2 g	**Fiber:**	8.2 g		

QUICK BALSAMIC
Quinoa Salad

Quinoa and pine nuts add a crunch, while corn adds a pinch of something sweet. And in my world, there's nothing better than a little olive oil and balsamic vinegar, with a dose of salt and pepper.

INGREDIENTS

1	Cup	Cooked quinoa
1	Cup	Frozen or fresh corn
⅓	Cup	Pine nuts
1	Large bowl	Lettuce
2	Tbsp.	Olive oil
1	Tbsp.	Balsamic vinegar
¼	Inch	Diced avocado (optional)
		Salt and pepper
½	Cup	Cherry tomato

INSTRUCTIONS

1. Heat a little olive oil in a pan, reduce the heat before adding the cooked quinoa, corn and pine nuts. Sauté until quinoa is slightly crisp, corn is slightly brown and pine nuts are toasted, about 5 to 10 minutes, stirring constantly.

2. Let the mixture cool to room temperature or slightly warmer and sprinkle with lettuce.

3. Beat the oil and vinegar, add salt and pepper to taste and add to the salad. Try adding more oil, vinegar or salt as desired.

4. Garnish with tomato, avocado, and top with grilled chicken breast if desired.

Nutrition

Calories:	179	Carbohydrates:	13.6 g	Protein:	3.9 g
Fat:	13.1 g	Fiber:	2.0 g		

FARRO SALAD

with Grilled Eggplant, Caramelized Onion and Pine Nuts

The aubergines grilled in-season reveal their rich silky and natural sweetness. Here, it shines in a simple but aromatic salad with thick farro seeds. Fresh or dry mint adds layers of flavor. Do not be intimidated by a few steps: this combination comes together effortlessly.

INGREDIENTS

For farro:

2	Cups	Water
1	Cup	Farro or about 3 cups cooked farro
2		Bay leaves
1		Dried red pepper, optional
1	Tsp.	Serrano ground green pepper, optional
¾	Tsp.	Aleppo pepper, or more as needed
1	Tsp.	Dried mint

For the salad:

1	Pound	Eggplant, cut into ¼-inch cubes (about 8 cups)
½		Medium red onion, thinly sliced (less than ¼-inch)
4	Tbsp.	Extra-virgin olive oil
½	Tsp.	Fine sea salt
½	Cup	Lightly chopped and torn fresh mint leaves
2	Tbsp.	White balsamic vinegar or red wine vinegar
⅓	Cup	Lightly toasted pine nuts

INSTRUCTIONS

1. Place the rack in the middle of the oven and preheat to 425° F.

2. To make the farro, add water, bay leaf, and dried chili to a 2-quart thick pan and bring to a boil. Reducing the heat to low, cover, and cook until the beans boil, let boil for 10 to 25 minutes. Remove the bay leaf and chili, drain if necessary and transfer to a large bowl. Sprinkle with ground pepper, Aleppo pepper, and mix with dry mint and onion.

3. Meanwhile, to make the salad, place the eggplant and onion on a baking sheet. Wash it with 2 tablespoons of olive oil, sprinkle with salt and mix thoroughly. If you don't mind an extra plate, it's a little easier to throw everything in a large bowl.

4. Cook the mixture until the eggplant pieces are soft and golden brown in places, and the onion slices are caramelized, turning them with a spatula for 30 to 35 minutes. Remove the baking sheet from the oven and immediately sprinkle the vegetables with ¼ cup of fresh mint and drizzle with 1 tablespoon of vinegar. Spread well—this will soften the mint leaves and remove the bite of vinegar.

5. Finally, add the hot eggplant mixture to the farro. Drizzle the remaining 2 tablespoons of olive oil and 1 tablespoon of vinegar and stir to combine. Season with salt and vinegar to taste. Garnish with ¼ cup of mint and remaining pine nuts and serve.

Nutrition

Calories:	200	Carbohydrates:	18.6 g	Protein:	4.1 g
Fat:	13.4 g	Fiber:	5.7 g		

TOMATO
and Feta Salad

Nothing better than a meal which comes together in minutes, especially on busy weekdays. Depending on the occasion, this delicious gluten-free recipe can be used as a main or side dish. You're free to pair with grilled meat or fish. Either way you want to enjoy it, it is definitely a summer dish.

Serves: 2 to 4

INGREDIENTS

2	Tbsp.	Olive oil
1	Tbsp.	Red wine vinegar
1	Tsp.	Minced shallot
		Pinch kosher salt
		Pinch freshly ground black pepper
1	Pint	Cherry or grape tomatoes (about 2 cups), halved
3	Oz.	Feta cheese, crumbled (about 1 cup)
¼	Cup	Coarsely chopped fresh parsley leaves
2	Tbsp.	Chopped fresh oregano leaves
3	Cups	mixed greens
½	Cup	cucumber, ¼ inch sliced
1		Small red onion, thinly sliced

INSTRUCTIONS

1. Whisk together the oil, vinegar, shallots and a generous pinch of salt and pepper in a large bowl. Add the mixed greens, cucumber, red onion, parsley and tomatoes.

2. Garnish with feta and oregano.

3. Season with more salt and pepper as needed.

Nutrition

Calories:	324	**Carbohydrates:**	20.4 g	**Protein:**	13.1 g
Fat:	17 g	**Fiber:**	8 g		

HEARTY SALAD
from the Farmers Market

Make sure you have a salad evening at least once a week because whatever you eat at the farmers market, this summer touch of a classic cobb will be your new favorite.

Fill your bowl with great fresh local dishes! Add a hard-boiled egg from the local farmer and taste new cheeses.

INGREDIENTS

For the dressing:

⅓	Cup	White wine vinegar
1		Garlic clove, minced
2	Tbsp.	Finely chopped fresh herbs such as parsley, basil, tarragon, dill, mint
1	Tbsp.	Dijon mustard
½	Tsp	Kosher salt
¼	Tsp	Freshly ground black pepper
½	Cup	Olive oil

For the salad:

1		Medium green leaf lettuce (about 8 ounces)
2		Medium tomatoes
1		Large cucumber
1		Medium corn on the cobb, peeled
4		Medium radishes
1		Medium avocado
4	Oz	Bacon, sliced, cooked and chopped
3		Hard-boiled eggs, cut in half
½	Cup	Crumbled blue cheese

INSTRUCTIONS – *For the vinaigrette (dressing):*

1. Whisk all ingredients in a small bowl until well combined, keep aside.

Making the salad:

2. Divide the lettuce leaves into thin ½-inch strips and transfer into a large bowl.

3. Using a small knife, core and dice tomatoes into smaller portions; place in the bowl.

4. Next, peel the cucumber, cut into cubes and transfer to the bowl. Remove the corn kernels from the cob, and transfer into the bowl.

5. Finely chop the radishes then add to the bowl.

6. Divide the avocado, cut into ½-inch cubes and place in bowl. Place the eggs and cheese in the bowl; garnish with bacon.

7. Sprinkle salad with dressing and mix well.

8. Enjoy!

Nutrition

Calories:	678	**Carbohydrates:** 17.6 g		**Protein:**	17.9 g
Fiber:	6.1 g				

MEDITERRANEAN COUSCOUS
Cauliflower Salad

One of the adored vegetables we grow (on our farm) is cauliflower. We won't be harvesting anytime soon, but the majority of the farms in our valley are already enjoying the fruits of this magnificent brassica. I was so excited to receive some!

INGREDIENTS

For the chickpeas:

1	Cup	Drained chickpeas
1	Tbsp.	Olive oil
¼	Tsp.	Cumin powder
½	Tsp.	Salt
⅛	Tsp.	Cayenne pepper

For the dressing:

2	Tbsp.	Freshly squeezed lemon juice
1		Garlic clove, minced
½	Tsp.	Dijon mustard
½	Tsp.	Salt
¼	Cup	Extra-virgin olive oil

For the salad:

1		Large cauliflower, in ½-inch florets
1 ½	Cups	Cherry tomatoes, halved
½		Medium red onion, diced
⅓	Cup	Pitted kalamata olives, finely chopped
1		English cucumber, finely chopped and peeled
1	Cup	Chopped fresh parsley
½	Cup	Pine nuts
¼	Tsp.	Red pepper flakes
		Salt and pepper

INSTRUCTIONS

1. Grill the chickpeas: Place the rack in middle of oven and preheat to 400° F.

2. Add all the chickpea ingredients into a medium bowl and mix. Transfer to a baking sheet lined with parchment paper and spread in a single layer. Make sure to roast until crisp. Stir after 30 minutes and if needed, continue to cook until they are nice and crisp.

3. Prepare the vinaigrette dressing: Add the lemon juice, mustard, garlic and salt in a small bowl and stir well. Add the olive oil and continue stirring until homogeneous. Taste the seasoning and adjust if necessary.

4. Making the salad: Place the cauliflower bouquets in the food processor with blade well placed. Pulse until you have a nice smooth consistency that always has a good bite! Make sure you don't press too hard and make it puréed.

5. Transfer the cauliflower into a large bowl. Add the rest of the salad ingredients and mix. Sprinkle with salad dressing. Season with salt and pepper as you desire. Garnish with grilled chickpeas and serve.

Nutrition

Calories:	410	**Carbohydrates:** 46.1 g		**Protein:**	15.3 g
Fat:	20.9g	**Fiber:**	11.0 g		

KALE SALAD
with Garlic Croutons

This salad is perfect for your friends and family having a barbecue this weekend! You'll feel good as long as you eat healthily!

INGREDIENTS

For the salad:

2		Bunches of kale, washed and dried
3	Tbsp.	Grapeseed oil or olive oil, divided
½	Tsp.	Salt and more for bread
2	Thick slices	Sourdough bread (about ¾-inch thick)
1		Small garlic clove
2	Tbsp.	Shaved parmesan (optional, see recipe notes)

For the dressing:

1		Medium garlic clove
2	Tbsp.	Lemon juice
½	Tsp.	Salt
2	Tbsp.	Extra-virgin olive oil

INSTRUCTIONS

1. Cut off the stem of each kale leaf.

2. In large bowl, mix the kale with 2 tablespoons of grapeseed oil and a little salt. Brush both sides of the bread with the rest of the grapeseed oil and sprinkle with salt.

3. Apply the garlic on each side of the bread.

4. Preheat a grill or pan over medium heat. Grill the kale leaves in small batches until golden and crisp, about 30 to 45 seconds per side.

5. Grill the bread until it is nice and charred on the both sides. Cut the kale leaves into ¾-inch pieces and place into a large bowl. Cut the bread into cubes of the desired size and set aside.

6. For the dressing: Using a grater, finely grate the garlic clove and mix with ¼ teaspoon of salt and lemon juice in a small bowl. Slowly add the olive oil. Pour dressing over chopped kale and toss evenly. Add or transfer into a serving bowl and garnish with garlic croutons.

Nutrition

Calories:	286	**Carbohydrates:** 31.5 g		**Protein:**	10.0 g
Fiber:	3.8 g				

DELICIOUS
Summer Salad

Have a great summer day, have lunch with your friends and dream of a great light meal. Well, this salad goes perfectly with it! Bold flavors, bright colors and great texture!

Serves: 2

INGREDIENTS

For the dressing:

¼	Cup	White wine vinegar
1		Small garlic clove, minced
1	Tsp.	Dijon mustard
½	Cup	Olive oil
		Salt and freshly ground pepper
1	Pinch	Cayenne pepper

For the salad:

2		Large eggs
½	Lb.	Potatoes
4	Oz.	Green beans
1	Can	Tuna packed in oil, drained (see recipe note)
2		Medium Italian tomatoes, cut into wedges
3	Cups	Lettuce
⅓	Cup	Nicoise olives
		Anchovy fillets (optional)
		Finely sliced red radish (optional)

INSTRUCTIONS

1. Prepare the dressing: Whisk the vinegar, chopped garlic, salt, pepper and mustard in a small bowl. Pour the oil into a slow, steady stream, stirring continuously until the dressing is well mixed.

2. Boil the eggs: Add the eggs into a small saucepan and cover with water. Cook over high heat to boil the water, turn off the heat, cover the pan and let stand 8 to 10 minutes. Drain the water and place the eggs in an ice bath to cool, peel and divide the eggs. Keep aside.

3. Cooking the potatoes: Add the potatoes into a medium saucepan and cover using cold water. Next, add 1 tablespoon of salt, and bring to a boil. Cook until the potatoes become tender, about 12–15 minutes. Take out the potatoes and drain, allow to cool for a few minutes.

4. Boil the green beans: Boil the water and add the green beans. Cook 3 to 4 minutes until light green and crisp. Remove the beans with a slotted spoon and transfer into an ice bath.

5. Dress the greens: In a large bowl, add the salad greens. Sprinkle a small amount of vinaigrette (dressing) around the greens and mix until completely covered. Divide the greens among the plates.

6. Cut the potatoes into ½-inch slices: Mix the potatoes in a small bowl with two tablespoons of dressing.

7. Arrange the rest of the ingredients and begin assembling the salad. Once you are done tossing the ingredients, put them on the plates and arrange them in sections, then place the tuna around the salad.

Nutrition

Calories:	398.2	Carbohydrates:	39.1 g	Protein:	23 g
Fat:	18.7 g	Fiber:	9.2 g		

FENNEL AND ARUGULA SALAD
with Lemon Vinaigrette

It only takes a few seconds to prepare this salad! You can serve with grilled salmon or brunch casserole – this arugula salad goes well with everything on the table.

INGREDIENTS

1	Tsp.	Lemon zest
2	Tbsp..	Juice of one lemon
¼	Tsp.	Salt
5	Oz.	Arugula, washed and dried
¾		Fennel bulb, shaved
2	Tbsp.	Extra-virgin olive oil
		Freshly ground pepper, to taste
		Pecorino, to serve
¼	Cup	Almonds or walnuts

INSTRUCTIONS

1. Combine arugula and shaved fennel in a bowl and refrigerate to keep it crisp.

2. In a small bowl, combine the olive oil, lemon zest, lemon juice, salt and pepper and mix well until blended.

3. Sprinkle dressing over the salad. Shave a few slices of pecorino on the salad. Decorate with almonds or nuts. Adding fresh apple slices is also great!

4. Serve immediately.

Nutrition

Calories:	398.2	Carbohydrates:	30.1 g	Protein:	29.0 g
Fat:	18 g	Fiber:	7.2 g		

CUCUMBER AND TOMATO

Caprese Salad

***Y**ou've got to try this refreshing salad. The flavor of cucumber mixed with the cheese flavor will bring your taste buds to life!*

INGREDIENTS

1	Lb.	Heirloom or beefsteak tomatoes (about 3 medium), cut to ¼-inch thick
1 ¼	Cup	Fresh mozzarella, cut into circles
½	Cup	Black olives
1	Head	Baby iceberg lettuce
		Extra-virgin olive oil
		Balsamic vinegar
		Sea salt (flaky)
		Freshly ground black pepper
		5 to 7 large fresh basil leaves

INSTRUCTIONS

1. Divide the iceberg lettuce into ¾-inch pieces. Place in the center of the plate and form a tower.

2. Next, lay out the tomato, olives and mozzarella slices over the tower. Sprinkle with olive oil and vinegar, salt and pepper.

3. Cut the basil leaves into small pieces and sprinkle over salad.

Nutrition

Calories:	232	**Carbohydrates:**	5.8 g	**Protein:**	9.2 g
Fiber:	4.2 g				

RAINBOW
Fruit Salad

Enjoy this healthy and yummy salad recipe – it contains all the colors of the rainbow, and offers much more than any regular type of salad.

INGREDIENTS

2	Tbsp.	Freshly squeezed lime juice (about 1 lime)
2	Tbsp.	Honey
1	Tbsp.	Mint leaves, freshly chopped
1	Small	Rainbow radish, very thinly sliced
1		Avocado, sliced into $1/8$ inch slices
1	Cup	Broccoli. ½ inch florets
1	Cup	Quinoa, cooked.

INSTRUCTIONS

1. In a medium size bowl, mix the lime juice and honey until fully blended. Add in all the vegetables and fold together.

2. Toss gently until fully combined. Garnish with mint and serve.

Nutrition

Calories:	87	**Carbohydrates:**	22.3 g	**Protein:**	1.1 g
Fat:	0.4 g	**Fiber:**	2.6 g		

FIRE GRILLED VEGETABLES

This amazing dish is best served directly from the grill, dressed in a warm vinaigrette, soaking up the delicious aromas. Let cool a few minutes before adding feta and mint for best results. This recipe works with all kinds of favorite vegetables! Tomatoes, asparagus, peppers, radishes, onions and even corn on the cob!

INGREDIENTS

3	Lbs.	Various vegetables; corn, zucchini, tomato, radish, green beans, red onion, bell peppers
4	Tbsp.	Olive oil, divided
		Finely grated zest of 1 medium lemon
2	Tbsp.	Freshly squeezed lemon juice
¼	Tsp.	Dried oregano
1	Tsp.	Kosher salt, divided
		Freshly ground black pepper
1	Cup	Crumbled feta cheese (optional)
1	Tbsp.	Chopped fresh mint leaves

INSTRUCTIONS

1. Apply maximum heat to a grill pan (cast iron works best). In the meantime, prepare the zucchini and all the other vegetables you like!

2. Thinly cut the zucchini into ¼-inch slices and place them into a large bowl.

3. Combine 3 tablespoons of oil, lemon zest, lemon juice, oregano and ¼ teaspoon of salt in a small bowl. Whisk together and keep aside.

4. When the grill has heated up, sprinkle the zucchini with the remaining 2 tablespoons of oil, drizzle with 1 teaspoon of salt, pepper and mix well. Lay them out in a pan or grill.

5. Cover and grill, turning occasionally if necessary until crisp and charred in places.

6. Put the squash in a bowl, sprinkle with vinaigrette (dressing) and mix. Let cool at a slightly warm or room temperature. Add the feta cheese and the mint, then slowly toss to combine.

Nutrition

Calories:	198	**Carbohydrates:** 10.3 g		**Protein:**	6 g
Fat:	16.3 g	**Fiber:**	3.1 g		

SALAD WITH MARINATED BEET
and Feta Cheese

Beet salad sounds like a plain dish, but there are numerous reasons for its popularity. When the hard beets are roasted soft and sweet and then mixed with a vinaigrette, something really amazing happens and that's what makes this dish so good!

INGREDIENTS

2	Lbs.	Beets
2	Tbsp.	Extra-virgin olive oil and more to sprinkle
1	Tbsp.	Finely chopped shallot
1	Cup	Arugula
		Finely grated zest of 1 medium lemon
1	Tbsp.	Freshly squeezed lemon juice
1	Tbsp.	Champagne or white wine vinegar
½	Tsp.	Dijon mustard
¼	Tsp.	Kosher salt
		Fresh ground black pepper, to taste
¼	Cup	Fresh, smooth herbs, cut into large pieces such as dill, parsley or mint (or a combination), divided
1 ¼	Cup	Feta cheese, cut into ¼-inch thick plates

INSTRUCTIONS

1. Place a rack in the center of the oven and preheat to 400° F.

2. Scrub the beets well and wrap them in aluminum foil. Smaller beets may be fine together, but wrapping large beets separately is always the best. Do not allow them to dry off after washing because this water prevents them from drying out during cooking.

3. Roast for 50 to 60 minutes until tender and easily pierced by knife. Check every 20 minutes or so. Meanwhile, prepare the dressing.

4. Add the oil, lemon zest, lemon juice, vinegar, shallots, mustard, salt and pepper in a large bowl and set aside.

5. Reserve the roasted beets until they are cold enough. Place one of the beets on a paper towel or tea towel and rub the skin off. Normally, the skin is easy to remove or peel off; otherwise, the beets may need a little longer to cook.

6. Slice the beets into wedges, ½-inch thick. Combine the beets and the dressing and mix well. After cooling, add half the herbs and toss to combine.

7. Distribute the ingredients on the plate and sprinkle the cheese and herbs over the salad. Drizzle with dressing and garnish with fresh arugula.

Nutrition

Calories:	209	Carbohydrates:	17.0g	Protein:	7.9 g
Fat:	12.8 g	Fiber:	4.5 g		

CARAMELIZED VEGETABLES

in a Sweet Vinegar

Roasted veggies, a tasty vegetarian salad that comes together in few minutes. Combine with a few thick slices of crusty bread to complete it. It is definitely a salad for your weekly winter dinner.

INGREDIENTS

2	Lb.	Sweet potatoes, peeled and 1/2 inch sliced. (you can also use corn, eggplant, peppers)
1	Lb.	Cremini mushrooms, halved or quartered when large
4		Medium shallots, peeled and quartered
3	Tbsp.	Olive oil
		Kosher salt
		Freshly ground black pepper
4		1 inch pieces of corn on the cob
4	Oz.	Fresh goat cheese, crumbled (about 1 cup)
¾	Cup	Roasted pumpkin seeds

For the dressing:

⅓	Cup	Extra-virgin olive oil
¼	Cup	Balsamic vinegar
2	Tsp.	Dijon mustard
1		Small garlic clove, grated or minced
½	Tsp.	Kosher salt
		Freshly ground black pepper

INSTRUCTIONS

1. Place rack in middle of the oven, and heat to 425° F.

2. Place sweet potatoes, shallots and mushrooms onto a baking sheet. Sprinkle with olive oil, a good pinch of salt and black pepper, and mix gently. Spread in an even layer.

3. Cook until smooth and slightly caramelized, stirring each 15 minutes. Meanwhile, prepare the dressing. Put all the ingredients into a small bowl and stir well.

4. In a large bowl, add the roasted vegetables. Sprinkle with about half of the dressing and spread evenly. Fold in the kale. Sprinkle with pumpkin seeds together with goat cheese

5. Serve while hot. Enjoy!

Nutrition

Calories:	508	**Carbohydrates:** 47.0 g	**Protein:**	15.4 g
Fat:	30.9 g	**Fiber:**	8.4 g	

CAESAR SALAD
with Broccoli and Kale

You can't afford to miss out on this delicious Mediterranean salad! A satisfying bowl of broccoli and kale, golden croutons, white beans and the best vegan Caesar dressing you've ever tasted.

INGREDIENTS

For the croutons:

4	Oz	Stale bread (about ½ medium baguette)
4	Tbsp.	Extra-virgin olive oil, divided
		Kosher salt
		Parsley
1	Tbsp.	Garlic powder (optional)

For the salad

1		Large broccoli (about 1 pound), cut into florets
4		Small garlic cloves, unpeeled
1		Medium kale (about 12 ounces), no broken stems and leaves
1	Can (15 oz)	Cannellini beans, drained and rinsed
¼	Cup	Fresh parsley leaves, chopped
½	Cup	Roasted sunflower seeds

For the dressing:

1	Cup	Cashews, salted or raw
¾	Cup	Low-sodium vegetable broth or water
2	Tbsp.	Extra-virgin olive oil
2	Tsp.	Capers
2	Tsp.	Freshly squeezed lemon juice
		Kosher salt

INSTRUCTIONS

1. Prepare the croutons and roast the broccoli: Set the oven rack and preheat to 400° F.

2. Divide the bread into ½-inch cubes. Place on a baking sheet, sprinkle with 1½ tablespoon of oil and season with salt. Spread in an even layer. Bake and if needed, continue to stir until all sides are evenly browned. Place in a bowl lined with paper towels and let cool.

3. Next, position the broccoli florets and the unpeeled garlic cloves on the same baking sheet. Sprinkle with 1½ tablespoons of oil and spread evenly. Grill the broccoli until golden and season with salt.

4. *For the dressing:* Squeeze the garlic out of their skins and place in a blender. Drain the water from the cashews and pour into the blender. Add the broth or water, oil, capers and lemon juice. Blend until smooth, adding salt and pepper as desired.

5. *Prepare the salad:* Add kale, 1 tablespoon of oil and a pinch of salt into a large bowl. Coat well and let stand for at least 5 minutes. Add roasted broccoli, cannellini beans and croutons and dressing, then mix well to combine. Garnish with parsley and sunflower seeds.

Nutrition

Calories:	677	Carbohydrates:	65.2 g	Protein:	24.6 g
Fat:	39.7 g	**Fiber:**	13.9 g		

SPICY PANZANELLA

Panzanella is an inexpensive bowl that turns hard bread that is difficult to consume into a tasty sponge, which even picky children enjoy. You can prepare this with a spicy vinaigrette for that extra kick!

INGREDIENTS

2		Large tomatoes, finely chopped
1		English cucumber (optional)
		Salt and pepper to taste
4–5	Slices	Day-old bread
2	Tbsp.	Olive oil plus a few drops for the pan
1		Medium jalapeño, finely chopped
		Salt and pepper to taste
1	Lime	Juice of one lime

Optional additions

		Fresh chopped herbs
		Peaches, nectarines or chopped plums
		Finely chopped red onion
		Chopped zucchini or summer squash
		Pitted olives
		Grapes

INSTRUCTIONS

1. Keep aside 2 tablespoons of finely chopped tomatoes for dressing.

2. Put the rest of the tomatoes and all the cucumbers into a large bowl. Sprinkle with salt and pepper, stir and set aside.

3. In a saucepan over medium heat, add a few drops of olive oil. Add the jalapeño and sauté until it sizzles. Add the rest of the chopped tomato and a tablespoon of water. Cook the tomato for around 2 minutes. Sprinkle with salt and pepper. As soon as the water evaporates, cut it very finely and mix it with the lime juice and 2 tablespoons of olive oil. Stir well, add salt and pepper accordingly.

4. Cut the bread into small pieces, then toast in a pan or skillet over medium heat, stirring occasionally until the bread chunks are toasted on all sides.

5. Combine the bread, dressing and vegetables. Add more salt and pepper as desired.

Nutrition					
Calories:	181	**Carbohydrates:** 24.9 g		**Protein:**	5.0 g
Fat:	8.1 g	**Fiber:**	3.6 g		

15-MINUTE BROILED SALMON

with Lemon, Mustard & Herbs

This awesome recipe can be made in under 15 minutes, which makes it ideal for the middle of the week when you have no time to prepare dinner yourself. Believe me, once you start sprinkling mustard, rosemary and chopped fresh thyme on the fillets, they will suddenly feel classy.

Serves: 4

INGREDIENTS

1	Tsp	Olive oil
4	5–6 Oz.	Salmon fillets
4	Tbsp.	Dijon mustard
2	Tsp.	Chopped fresh rosemary leaves
1	Tsp.	Chopped fresh thyme leaves
1	Tsp.	Oregano
1	Tsp.	Kosher salt
¼	Tsp.	Freshly ground black pepper
1		Medium lemon

INSTRUCTIONS

1. Set your oven to broil and insert a rack about 6 inches from the broiler. Line a baking sheet with aluminum foil.
2. Rub oil over the salmon to evenly distribute. Lay the salmon skin side down on the prepared baking sheet.
3. Combine Dijon mustard, thyme, oregano, rosemary, salt and pepper in a small bowl. Distribute the mixture evenly over the salmon fillets and coat accordingly.
4. Broil for about 6 to 8 minutes until the salmon is cooked through. I recommend that you cook the salmon to a medium temperature, 135° F, so it remains moist. Squeeze half the lemon over the salmon and serve.
5. Place the salmon on a bed of Romain lettuce and serve with sliced cucumbers and tomatoes.

Nutrition

Calories:	376	Carbohydrates:	1.7 g	Protein:	35.4 g
Fat:	24.5 g	Fiber:	0.9 g		

FISH IN TOMATO SAUCE

with herbs

Are you tired of eating tomatoes raw, but want them fresher than in a slow-cooked sauce? This recipe is perfect for late summer! This recipe is perfect for late summer!

Fresh tomatoes simmered with garlic and herbs make this a perfect lighter selection for a late night meal.

INGREDIENTS

2	Tbsp.	Olive oil
2		Garlic cloves, minced
¼	Tsp.	Red pepper flakes
1 ½	Lb	Ripe tomatoes (about 5 medium), cut into 1-inch pieces
3	Cups	Water
1	Tbsp.	Chopped fresh oregano leaves
1	Tbsp.	Chopped fresh thyme leaves
		Kosher salt
		Freshly ground pepper to taste
1 ½	Lbs.	Red basa or tilapia fillets. Cut them into 4 pieces.

INSTRUCTIONS

1. Heat the oil in a deep skillet over medium heat until it shines or shimmers. Add garlic, red pepper flakes and cook (sauté) until the garlic begins to turn golden brown, around 10 seconds.

2. Add water, tomatoes, oregano and thyme and bring to a boil. Cover and simmer for 15 minutes. Take out the lid, lower the heat to medium and simmer for additional 8 to 10 minutes to thicken the sauce. Season with salt and pepper as desired.

3. Return the fish to the pan, season with salt, cover and cook for another 7 to 9 minutes or until the fish becomes tender.

4. Put a piece of fish with sauce in 4 separate bowls.

5. Serve immediately.

Nutrition

Calories:	270	**Carbohydrates:**	8.9 g	**Protein:**	36.8 g
Fat:	9.5 g	**Fiber:**	3.0 g		

BRAISED COD SKILLET

with Asparagus and Potatoes

As you know already, braising is one of our favorite methods of cooking fish. With this recipe, you will get juicy and tender fillets. The juicy flavor of the fish mixed with the aroma of basil ensures that nothing is left on the plate!

INGREDIENTS

2	Tbsp.	Olive oil
4		Skinless cod fillets (3/4-inch thick) (6 to 8 oz each)
3		Garlic cloves, thinly sliced
2	Tbsp.	Capers
		Finely grated zest of 1 medium lemon
½	Cup	Dry white wine
2	Cups	Water
12	Oz.	Small purple potatoes, cut in half or quartered when large
½		Medium lemon juice
½	Tsp.	Kosher salt and more for seasoning
½	Tsp.	Freshly ground black pepper and more as a condiment
1	Pound	Asparagus, cut and trimmed into 1-inch pieces
¼	Cup	Grated fresh basil leaves

INSTRUCTIONS

1. Slowly apply oil in a large skillet pan over medium heat until it shimmers (shines). Season the fish with salt and pepper as desired. Add the fish to the pan and fry for 1 minute. Gently flip or rotate with a flat spatula and sear for another 1 minute. Bring the fish onto a plate and set it aside.

2. Add the garlic, capers and lemon zest to the pan. Mix to coat with the remaining oil in pan and cook until fragrant, for 1 minute.

3. Add wine and deglaze the pan with a spoon (preferably wooden) to scrape off all the browned parts from the bottom of the pan. Add water, potatoes, lemon juice, ½ teaspoon salt and ¼ teaspoon pepper. Bring to a boil, lower the heat and simmer uncovered for 10 to 12 minutes until the potatoes are tender.

4. Add the asparagus and cook for 2 minutes. Bring back the cod fillets and juices to the pan. Cook until the fish is opaque and warm and the asparagus is tender, for another 2–3 minutes.

5. Separate the fish fillets in flat bowls and place the potatoes and asparagus in the bowls. Add the basil to the broth in the pan and pour broth across the fish. Enjoy!

Nutrition

Calories:	136.9	**Carbohydrates:** 13.9 g		**Protein:**	18.6 g
Fat:	0.2 g	**Fiber:**	0.4 g		

PUTTANESCA
with Tuna

The tuna matches match perfectly with this recipe's sauce. Make a double batch and use the leftovers later in the week with the pasta as entrée dish!

INGREDIENTS

4		Tuna steaks (6 ounces each)
½	Tsp.	Salt
¼	Tsp.	Black pepper
1	Tbsp.	Olive oil
3		Garlic cloves, minced
1	Can	Anchovy fillets, drained and cut into pieces
1	14.5-oz. can	Diced tomatoes
¼	Cup	Pitted kalamata olives, chopped
2	Tbsp.	Capers, drained
¼	Tsp.	Ground red pepper (or to taste)
2	Tbsp.	Chopped parsley

INSTRUCTIONS

1. Apply salt and pepper to season the fish.

2. Over medium heat in a non-stick skillet, heat the oil. Add the fish and cook for 3 to 4 minutes on each side or until the desired cooking point is reached. Remove from pan and loosely cover with aluminum foil to keep warm.

3. Add the garlic and anchovies, and cook, stirring for 1 minute until the garlic is no longer raw. Add the tomatoes, olives, capers and chopped red pepper and cook, stirring occasionally, for about 2 minutes until the tomatoes begin to dissolve. Sprinkle the fish with parsley and enjoy!

Nutrition

Calories:	549.1	**Carbohydrates:** 75.4 g		**Protein**	21.7 g
Fat:	18.2 g				

SIMPLE AND HEALTHY

Greek Salmon Salad

So many things make this recipe unique among other Greek salads. For example, it uses butter lettuce instead of romaine, and the raw onion is dipped in cold water to tame the bite. The combination of flavors gives life and taste to common vegetables that people avoid.

INGREDIENTS

¼	Cup	Olive oil
3	Tbsp.	Red wine vinegar
2	Tbsp.	Freshly squeezed lemon juice (from 1 lemon)
1		Garlic clove, minced
¾	Tsp.	Dried oregano
½	Tsp.	Kosher salt
¼	Tsp.	Freshly ground black pepper
½		Small red onion, thinly sliced
¼	Cup	Cold water
4	6-oz. fillets	Skinless salmon
2		Medium heads of butter lettuce like Boston or bibb (about 1 pound), cut into small pieces
2		Medium tomatoes, cut into 1-inch pieces
1		Medium English cucumber, quartered lengthwise, then cut into ½-inch pieces
½	Cup	Pitted kalamata olives, halved lengthwise
4	Oz.	Feta cheese, crumbled (about 1 cup)
4	Strips	Pre-cooked crispy bacon (optional)

INSTRUCTIONS

1. Begin by placing a rack in the center of the oven. Set to 425° F. While heating the oven, marinate the salmon and soak the onions.

2. In a bowl, mix and combine the olive oil, vinegar, lemon juice, garlic, oregano, salt and pepper. Use 3 tablespoons of dressing in a baking dish large enough to retain all the pieces of salmon in a single layer. Add the salmon and gently turn it over several times to coat the dressing well. Cover and refrigerate. Place the onion and water in a small container, set aside for 10 minutes to make the onion less strong. Drain and discard the liquid.

3. Uncover the salmon and roast for 8 to 12 minutes until cooked thoroughly. You'll notice a temperature of 120° F to 130° F in the center or middle of the thickest fillet for rare medium. However, if you need to cook it further, the thickest fillet should reach 135° F to 145° F. The total cooking time depends on the thickness of the salmon, based on the thickest part of the fillet. In the meantime, proceed and prepare the salad.

4. Combine the lettuce, tomato, cucumber, olives and drained red onions in the bowl with the dressing and spread evenly. Divide into 4 flat plates or bowls. When the salmon is ready, put 1 fillet on each salad. Sprinkle with feta and bacon.

5. Serve immediately.

Nutrition

Calories:	863.5	**Carbohydrates:**	17.6 g	**Protein:**	85.9 g
Fat:	49.9 g	**Fiber:**	4.3 g		

SKILLET FISH FILLET

with Lemon and Capers

This is a delicious recipe to enjoy, especially when the whole family gets together on the weekend. To prepare the crispy and golden fish, make sure that the fillets (fresh or frozen then thawed) are dry already. Dusting them lightly with flour gives them a very fine crust and also thickens them in the pan sauce. Although cod is suggested here, any thicker portion of white fish, whether tilapia, haddock or halibut, can be substituted and will provide the same amount of flavor.

INGREDIENTS

2	Tbsp	Olive oil
1	Lb.	Skinless cod fillets (about ½-inch thick), thawed from frozen and very dry
2	Tbsp.	All-purpose flour
½	Tsp.	Kosher salt
¼	Tsp.	Freshly ground black pepper
1		Medium lemon
⅓	Cup	Capers, drained
3	Tbsp.	Unsalted butter
2		Crushed garlic cloves
		Fresh parsley leaves torn, to serve

INSTRUCTIONS

1. Heat the oil until shimmering, in a large coated pan over medium heat. Next, sprinkle the cod evenly with flour, salt and pepper on each side. Place the cod fillets in the pan and fry until golden throughout, about 3 minutes on both sides. Transfer to a plate and cover with aluminum foil to keep them warm.

2. Once you have transfered the cod, gently increase the temperature and add in the lemon juice. As it begins to bubble add the capers, butter and garlic and stir over the heat until the butter is fully melted and fragrant, about 1 minute. Pour the sauce over the fish and sprinkle with parsley.

3. Serve immediately. Enjoy!

Nutrition

Calories:	253	**Carbohydrates:**	5.5 g	**Protein:**	21.2 g
Fat:	16.3 g	**Fiber:**	0.8 g		

GREEK STYLE
Tuna Salad

Having tuna salad, stuffed with mayonnaise and packed between two slices of wheat bread, inspires no one at all. With this awesome platter, you will surely make your taste buds dance. It's loaded with fresh vegetables and herbs, with no trace of sticky mayonnaise in sight!

INGREDIENTS

2	4 oz. cans	Tuna packed in oil, drained
⅓	Cup	Cherry tomatoes
½	Cup	Peeled cucumber
1	Cup	Mixed greens
2	Tbsp.	Coarsely chopped fresh oregano leaves
2	Tbsp.	Coarsely chopped fresh parsley leaves
3	Tbsp.	Olive oil
1	Tbsp.	Freshly squeezed lemon juice
		Kosher salt
		Freshly ground black pepper

INSTRUCTIONS

1. Add all the ingredients in a flat medium bowl and stir gently. Season with salt and pepper then taste. Add more seasoning as desired!

Nutrition

Calories:	225	**Carbohydrates:**	4.5 g	**Protein:**	21.4 g
Fat:	13.6 g	**Fiber:**	2.0 g		

INFALLIBLE SALMON

Baked with Olive Oil and Herbs

Are you always intimidated by fish? You may be afraid to overcook an expensive dinner. This method of cooking salmon is the gateway to improving your skills while providing a 5-star restaurant meal. There is no way to mess it up. The process is so easy and foolproof!

INGREDIENTS

¼	Cup Plus 2 Tbsp.	Olive oil
1 ¼	Lb.	Salmon fillet
		Sea salt and freshly ground black pepper flakes
1		Medium shallot, coarsely chopped (about ¼ cup)
⅓	Cup	Fresh dill, lightly chopped
¼	Cup	Fresh parsley or tarragon, lightly chopped
		Zest of 1 lemon

INSTRUCTIONS

1. Set oven to 250° F. Transfer ¼ cup olive oil into a medium baking pan, wide enough to contain all of the salmon. Place the salmon fillet skin side down in the olive oil. Season well with salt and pepper.

2. Combine the shallot, dill, parsley and lemon zest in a mincer (alternatively, use food processor or finely chop the shallot and spices and mix well with the other ingredients). Mix in 2 tablespoons of olive oil. Apply this herb paste across the entire salmon.

3. Bake the salmon for 25 minutes, depending on the density of the salmon fillet. Insert a fork into the thickest part of the steak and gently pull to verify the cooking. Easy flaking means the fish is done. If it is still sticky and the fork is difficult to remove, bake the salmon for an additional 5 minutes and check again.

4. For serving, carefully slip a spatula under the fish and place on a cutting board. Divide the fillet into four equal parts with a sharp knife.

5. Go ahead; serve with rice or fresh bread. Enjoy!

Nutrition

Calories:	489	**Carbohydrates:**	3.8 g	**Protein:**	29.6 g
Fat:	39.4 g	**Fiber:**	1.0 g		

MEDITERRANEAN
Tuna Fry

Each time I thought of making a lighter and healthier tuna noodle casserole, something as simple as my classic childhood favorite, my thoughts naturally turned to France.

INGREDIENTS

		Olive oil
10	Oz.	Wide, dry egg noodles or penne
1	Lb.	Small red potatoes, cut to ¼-inch thick
5	Tbsp.	Unsalted butter
¼	Cup	All-purpose flour
2	Cups	Milk
3	Tsp.	Kosher salt, divided
		Freshly ground black pepper
4	6-oz. cans	Tuna packed in olive oil, drained
1	8-oz. can	Artichoke hearts, thawed and cut in half
¾	Cup	Capers, rinsed and drained
½	Cup	Sliced black olives
4		Medium onions, thinly sliced
⅓	Cup	Fresh flat leaf parsley, finely chopped
¾	Cup	Parmesan cheese, finely grated, divided

INSTRUCTIONS

1. Position rack in the middle of the oven and preheat to 400° F. Coat a 2-liter or 9x13-inch baking pan with oil. Keep aside.

2. Bring a pot of salted water to a boil. Add noodles and cook for 2 minutes. Drain the noodles and add to a large bowl. Immediately mix with a drizzle of olive oil so they don't stick together; set aside.

3. Fill the pot with water and bring to a boil for a second time. Insert the potato slices and cook for 4 minutes. Drain properly and return to the pot.

4. While cooking the noodles and potatoes, heat the butter in a small saucepan over medium heat. When it melts and foams, add the flour and cook for about 5 minutes, stirring regularly. Add milk. Cook, stirring constantly, for about 5 minutes until the sauce thickens slightly. Add 1 teaspoon of salt and pepper to taste.

5. Transfer the noodles to the potato pot and pour the sauce over them. Mix in the remaining 1 teaspoon of salt, tuna, artichoke hearts, capers, olives, green onions, parsley and half a cup of Parmesan. Season with more salt as you like.

6. Place in a baking dish and spread evenly. Sprinkle with remaining ¼ cup of parmesan cheese. Bake for at least 25 minutes until foamy/bubbly. Serve hot immediately!

Nutrition

Calories:	745	**Carbohydrates:** 61.7 g		**Protein:**	51.7 g
Fat:	32.7 g	**Fiber:**	6.8 g		

SAUCY SALMON
Dinner

Have a soothing salmon dinner with sauce! It is cooked in a fresh tomato sauce garnished with garlic, balsamic vinegar and a touch of fresh thyme, which makes it slightly spicy. Once the salmon has absorbed as much flavorful juice as possible, the rest is left to the couscous on which it is served!

INGREDIENTS

2	Pints	Cherry tomatoes (about 20 oz or a total of 4 cups)
2		Crushed garlic cloves
3	Tbsp.	Olive oil, divided
2	Tsp.	Balsamic vinegar
2	Tsp.	Fresh thyme leaves
½	Tsp.	Kosher salt and more for seasoning
		Freshly ground black pepper
4	5-6 oz. fillets	Salmon, skin-on
		Cooked couscous, to serve

INSTRUCTIONS

1. Using a blender or food processor, add 1 tablespoon of oil, garlic, the tomatoes, vinegar, thyme, ¼ teaspoon of salt and a little ground black pepper. Blend well until saucy, set aside.

2. Use a clean paper towel or cloth to pat dry each salmon fillet on both sides to avoid sticking to pan. Season both sides with salt and pepper.

3. Heat the extra 2 tablespoons of oil in a large or medium size skillet pan covered with a lid until shimmering. Add the salmon, skin side down, to the pan and press down firmly so that the skin touches the pan uniformly and browns smoothly. Reduce heat to medium-low and cook without stirring. At regular intervals, gently press the fish until the sides are cooked nearly halfway, for 6 to 9 minutes, depending on the thickness of the fillets. Place the salmon fillets on a plate, skin side up.

4. Add the tomato mixture to the pan and bring to boil or simmer. Place the salmon in the pan and add the sauce. Cover and simmer for 2 to 5 minutes, depending on the thickness of the fillets.

5. Serve the salmon with lots of sauce on the cooked couscous. Enjoy your meal!

Nutrition

Calories:	482	**Carbohydrates:**	8.5 g	**Protein:**	36.5 g
Fat:	33.3 g	**Fiber:**	2.4 g		

ROASTED RED PEPPER AND BEET HUMMUS

This was a recipe that emerged as a spontaneous idea when I scanned the supermarket aisles just an hour before dinner. I saw hummus, we had vegetables at home, and I'd add some baguette. Bowls of hummus, basically a bunch of juicy vegetables with creamy hummus, have been so well received that they are now regularly on our meal planning list. This smoky and vibrant edition is the version I like the most!

INGREDIENTS

Hummus:

1		Red beet
2	Lg	Reg peppers
2	Cloves of garlic	
2	Tbsp	Garlic
2	Tbsp	Olive oil
1 ½	Cups	Cooked chickpeas, drained
2	Tbsp	Tahini
2	Tbsp	Lemon juice
2	Tbsp	Warm water
½	tsp	Cumin
½	tsp	Coriander
1	tsp	Salt
1	tsp	Pepper
1	tsp	Smoked paprika
1		French baguette
1		Clove garlic
2	Tbsp	Butter

INSTRUCTIONS

1. Preheat oven to 400 F. Coat the beet and red peppers in olive oil and garlic, wrap the beet in foil. Cook on baking sheet until the beet is fork-tender and the red peppers are starting to break down and become caramelized.

2. With 10 minutes left on the beet and red peppers, slice the french baguette into ¼ inch slices. Mix together the garlic and butter and spread across each piece. Add to the oven for the remaining time or until nice and crispy. Sprinkle with salt. Set aside.

3. While cooking, gather the rest of the ingredients and place in Robot Coupe or blender.

4. Once the beet and red peppers are ready, peel the beat and let them sit to cool. Add everything together and pulse until smooth. This will take about 3-5 minutes. Let cool in the fridge for 30 minutes.

5. Serve with the baguette and your favorite vegetables!

Nutrition

Calories:	376	Carbohydrates:	47 g	Protein:	18 g
Fat:	22 g	Fiber:	16.8 g		

VEGETABLE PIE (TART)

with Puff Pastry & Pesto

When you have puff pastry stored in the freezer, you can make some amazing things. This includes a tart pie with a colorful mosaic of summer vegetables, on fragrant basil pesto and sprinkled with a pinch of feta cheese and pepper flakes. A still warm portion of this buttery pie is exactly what you want to eat outside with a glass of iced rose wine.

INGREDIENTS

1	Lb.	Tomatoes (about 3 medium), cut in half
2	Medium	Zucchini or summer squash (about 10 ounces), cut into ¼-inch slices
1	Tsp.	Kosher salt
1	Packet	14 to 17 oz of frozen puff pastry (buttery type preferred), thawed in the refrigerator
½	Cup	Basil pesto at room temperature
3	Oz.	Feta cheese, crumbled (about ½ cup)
½	Tsp.	Red pepper flakes
		Freshly ground black pepper

INSTRUCTIONS

1. Get two medium plates or simply use a baking sheet and add the tomatoes and summer squash. Sprinkle with salt and let stand for 20 minutes. In the meantime, set up a rack in the oven. Preheat to 400° F.

2. Gather a baking sheet and parchment. Next, take the parchment to a fine working surface. Carefully unwind the pastry across the parchment paper (if your package contains 2 sheets, overlap them slightly so that they fit on the baking sheet). Use a rolling pin to roll out the pastry to form a rectangle, covering almost all of the baking sheet. Place the puff pastry onto the baking sheet, making sure you use the parchment paper to transfer everything over.

3. Gently roll about ½-inch on each side towards the middle to create the outer edge of the tart. Spread the pesto over the pastry for uniform distribution. Pat dry the vegetables with paper towels to absorb the damp moisture. Arrange the vegetable slices evenly over the pesto and overlap slightly to fit. Sprinkle with feta, pepper flakes and black pepper.

4. Bake 35 to 40 minutes until the edges are puffy and the bottom is golden. Cut into pieces and serve hot!

Nutrition

Calories:	321	**Carbohydrates:** 24.2 g		**Protein:**	5.7 g
Fat:	22.8 g	**Fiber:**	1.8 g		

ZUCCHINI PANCAKES
with Flavorful Carrots

I'm always looking for new ways to use my zucchini. I made zucchini crisps and sticks, but this time I wanted to try something simple, unique, and healthier. These pancakes are incredibly easy to prepare, low in calories and the perfect way to eat vegetables!

INGREDIENTS

1	Large	Zucchini
6	Medium	Carrots, peeled
1	Bunch	Chives
2	Cloves	Garlic
½	Bunch	Fresh parsley
1		Pancake batter recipe, like buttermilk pancakes

INSTRUCTIONS

1. Using a box grater, grate the zucchini and carrots. Cut the onions into thin slices, and finely chop the garlic and parsley.

2. Make a recipe for any pancake mix of your choice, but use ¼ cup less liquid than required. Zucchini will add a great deal of moisture to the mix. Next, mix the vegetables inside the prepared pancake batter.

3. Heat a skillet over medium temperature and brush lightly with olive oil. Use ⅓ measuring cup and scoop the batter in the heated skillet. Cook for 3 to 4 minutes until the outer edges are in place, then invert. Cook another 2 to 3 minutes and remove from the heat.

4. Sprinkle the pancakes with salt and let cool slightly before serving. Serve with butter or sour cream. Enjoy!

Nutrition

Calories:	100	**Carbohydrates:** 20.2 g		**Protein:**	3.6 g
Fat:	1.6 g	**Fiber:**	5.3 g		

PASTA AND VEGETABLES
with Lemon Butter

This pasta recipe takes what you already have available at home and transforms it into something exciting. Collect all the zucchini you can't dispose of, a pint of grape tomatoes, and plenty of fresh, fragrant basil from the garden, and make a light, sparkling, and relaxing dinner.

INGREDIENTS

1	Lb.	Dry pasta of your choosing
2	Tbsp	Olive oil
1	Cup	Spinich
¼	Cup	Bacon bits
1	Tsp.	Kosher salt and more for pasta water
½	Tsp.	Freshly ground black pepper
2	Tbsp.	Unsalted butter
2		Garlic cloves, minced
2	Tsp.	Finely grated lemon zest
3	Tbsp.	Freshly squeezed lemon juice
⅓	Cup	Fresh basil leaves, chopped
		Grated parmesan cheese to serve (optional)

INSTRUCTIONS

1. Over medium heat, bring a pot of salty water to a boil. Add the pasta and cook for one minute less than al dente. Meanwhile, cook the vegetables.

2. In a large skillet, heat the olive oil over medium heat until it begins to shimmer. Add spinnich and bacon. Season with salt and pepper. Cook until completely softened, about 4 to 5 minutes.

3. Next, add the garlic, lemon zest and butter. Cook until the butter is melted and fragrant, for 1 minute. Remove from heat and add lemon juice.

4. Preserve ½ cup of the pasta cooking water when you drain the pasta. Re-heat the skillet over medium heat. Add pasta and reserved cooking water and toss continuously until the sauce thickens and covers the pasta, 1 to 2 minutes. Taste and season with more salt and pepper as needed. Take off heat and add the basil. Garnish with parmesan to serve (optional).

Nutrition

Calories:	381	**Carbohydrates:** 62.1 g		**Protein:**	11.5 g
Fat:	9.9 g	**Fiber:**	4.0 g		

PARMESAN CHICKEN

with Kale Sauté

This healthy and special skillet dinner is a suitable meal for the weekdays. I think parmesan can improve almost any dish. Here, I'm referring to boneless chicken breasts and kale, two things that are sometimes hard to like, but trust me, you'll definitely like them here.

INGREDIENTS

2	Tbsp	Olive oil
1 ½	Lb.	Boneless, skinless chicken breast, cut into ½-inch strips
		Kosher salt
		Freshly ground black pepper
1	Medium	Yellow onion, diced
2		Garlic cloves, minced
1	Pinch	Red pepper flakes
1	Large	Bunch of kale (about 12 grams), chopped stems and leaves
½	Cup	Dry white wine
¾	Cup	Grated parmesan
1	Tbsp.	Freshly squeezed lemon juice

INSTRUCTIONS

1. In a skillet pan, preheat the oil until shimmering. Season the chicken with salt and pepper and add to the skillet. Cook for about 6 minutes. Place chicken on plate and cover to keep warm.

2. Next, add onion, garlic, and pepper flakes to skillet. Sauté for the next 2 minutes until the onions slightly soften. Add the kale, wine, and a pinch of salt. Cover and cook, stirring occasionally, for about 5 minutes, until the kale is tender.

3. Return chicken and all the juices to the skillet. Include both the parmesan and lemon juice; mix well. Season with more salt and pepper if you want!

Nutrition

Calories:	402	**Carbohydrates:**	12.9 g	**Protein:**	47.6 g
Fat:	15.7 g	**Fiber:**	3.9 g		

CHICKEN SALAD
with Vegetable Pesto

To make easy, fun and enjoyable salad, just mix up the way you prep the vegetables! Rather than the usual chunks or spears, this version of the recipe first cuts the zucchini into thin ribbons. With wavy zucchini ribbons, the salad immediately feels classy and it's easy to do with a mandolin or any regular peeler!

84

INGREDIENTS

For the pesto:

1	Cup	Fresh basil leaves, chopped
¾	Cup	Arugula
2	Tbsp.	Toasted nuts like pine nuts, walnuts, or cashews
3	Tbsp.	Grated parmesan
1	Clove	Garlic
½	Tsp.	Kosher salt
¼	Cup	Olive oil

For the salad:

½	Medium	Red onion, thinly sliced
1 ½	Lb.	Skinless, boneless chicken breast
1	Tbsp.	Olive oil
1 ¼	Cup	Green beans, cut
4	Small /Medium	Zucchini (about 1 ½ pounds total), trimmed
½	Pint	Cherry tomatoes, cut in half
		Kosher salt
		Freshly ground black pepper
½	Avocado	Cut into ¼-inch cubes (optional)

INSTRUCTIONS

1. **For the pesto:** Using a food processor or blender, add the cheese, basil, nuts and salt. Finely chop for about a minute. Scrape down the sides of the bowl. Add the oil as the processing device is in action and mix until the pesto is smooth. Keep aside.

2. **Prepare the salad:** Transfer the onion into a large basin or bowl, add 2 tablespoons of pesto and stir to combine. Keep aside.

3. Pat dry the chicken with paper towels and season well with salt and pepper, on both sides. In a medium or large skillet coated with oil, gently apply heat until shimmering. Add the chicken and cook gently until golden brown at the base, about 6 to 9 minutes. Rotate and cook until browned on second side and inside temperature reaches 165° F for 6 to 9 minutes. Place on clean cutting board and cover with foil.

4. Next, bring a pot of salted water to a boil. Insert the green beans and cook for about 2 minutes until crisp and tender. Drain and keep aside.

5. Using a vegetable peeler, Y peeler, or mandolin, cut the zucchini into approximately ¹⁄₁₆-inch ribbons from top to bottom. Transfer to the bowl with the onions. Coat using ⅓ of the remaining pesto.

6. Divide the chicken into 1-inch cubes. Add the rest of the pesto, chicken, green beans, and tomatoes to the bowl of vegetables and stir gently until evenly coated. Serve warm and enjoy!

Nutrition

Calories:	479	**Carbohydrates:** 14.8 g		**Protein:**	45.7 g
Fat:	27.0 g	**Fiber:**	4.9 g		

SOURDOUGH PORTOBELLO

Mushroom Sandwich

What does it take to have a good vegan sandwich? Numerous things are involved – prudent construction, good balance between textures and flavors and most importantly, bringing satisfaction without depending on meat or cheese! For good reasons, Portobello mushrooms are a popular choice of ingredient, and there's no exception in this recipe. Try toasting the bread to make it really enticing!

INGREDIENTS

1	Medium	Portobello mushroom (at least 3 ounces), finely scrubbed and stem removed
1	Tbsp.	Olive oil
		Salt
		Freshly ground black pepper
2	Tsp.	Balsamic vinegar
2	Slices	Sourdough bread or bun
1		Garlic clove, cut lengthwise in half
2	Tbsp.	Mayonnaise (vegan mayonnaise if desired)
½	Cup	Baby spinach leaves
⅓	Cup	Roasted pepper

INSTRUCTIONS

1. If necessary, scrape the black gills from the bottom of the mushroom and discard immediately (they're very bitter to the taste). Split the mushroom into ½-inch thick slices.

2. In a small frying pan, add the oil and gently apply heat until shimmering. Add the mushrooms, then season with salt and pepper. Cook for 5 to 6 minutes, stirring occasionally until everything turns golden brown. Sprinkle the vinegar over the mushrooms and stir. Cook for about 1 minute until the mushrooms completely absorb the vinegar. Remove pan from the fire.

3. Next, prepare and toast the bread. Rub the sliced side of the garlic on one side of the sliced bread. Spread a tablespoon of mayonnaise on each slice of bread. Add spinach, top with mushrooms and peppers.

4. Place the other slice of bread over the pepper and close the sandwich. Lightly press the sandwich to compress it, and cut in half with a serrated knife before serving.

Nutrition

Calories:	103	**Carbohydrates:**	9.5 g	**Protein:**	2.7 g
Fat:	6.3 g	**Fiber:**	1.2 g		

SOCCA PIZZA WITH RICOTTA
and Spring Veggies

Socca pizza is a well-known street food in Nice (France) that is prepared by combining chickpea flour and water to make a batter. Next, you cook the batter on a hot grill and finally shape or slice into smaller pieces. It is usually eaten hot and served simply with salt, pepper and a cold glass of dry rosé. You definitely have to try it out!

INGREDIENTS

For the socca:

1	Cup	Chickpea flour (4 ½ ounces)
1	Cup	Water
2	Tbsp.	Extra-virgin olive oil, plus more for the pan
1	Medium clove	Garlic, minced
1	Tsp.	Kosher salt

For topping:

½	Cup	Whole-milk ricotta cheese
½	Cup	Baby arugula
2	Medium	Radishes, thinly sliced
		Juice of 1 small lemon
		Finely grated zest of ½ small lemon
		Extra-virgin olive oil, flaky sea salt, and freshly ground black pepper, for finishing

INSTRUCTIONS

1. In a medium-size bowl, whisk the chickpea flour, water, olive oil, garlic and salt. Allow to rest at least 30 minutes to absorb the water.

2. Place the oven rack 6 inches below the heating element and preheat to 450° F. Place a 10-inch cast iron skillet in the oven for about 5 minutes.

3. Carefully remove the hot pan from the oven. Add about 1 teaspoon of oil, enough to cover the bottom of the pan. When it shimmers, pour the batter into the center of the pan. Tilt the pan so that the dough covers the entire surface of the pan if necessary.

4. Cook for 5 to 8 minutes until the top of the crust begins to brown. The crust should be soft enough in the center, but crunchy at the edges. If the top browns too quickly before the dough is completely hardened, place the pan on the lower rack until it is cooked through.

5. Pass the flat spatula under the crust, and remove it from the pan, and place on a cutting board. Spread the ricotta over it, leaving a border around the edges. Top with radishes.

6. Drizzle with lemon juice and olive oil and sprinkle with lemon zest, salt and pepper. Cut into rings and serve.

Nutrition

Calories:	163	Carbohydrates:	13.8 g	Protein:	6 g
Fat:	8.8 g	Fiber:	2.5 g		

ORZO SOUP
with Chicken and Lemon

Healthy Crockpot recipe, super light and family friendly! You have to try it. ***Equipment: Crockpot!***

INGREDIENTS

4		Skinless chicken breasts
2	Large	Carrots, peeled and sliced
2		Celery sticks, finely chopped
2	Cups	Chicken broth
4	Cups	Vegetable broth
4		Garlic cloves, minced
½	Tsp.	Dried basil
¾	Tsp.	Italian herbs
2		Bay leaves
1		Lemon, juiced (about 2 Tbsp)
		A handful of freshly ground parsley
1	Cup	Orzo
		Pepper and salt to taste

INSTRUCTIONS

1. Prepare the celery and carrots. Remove all fat from the chicken.
2. Cook all the ingredients excluding salt, pepper, lemon juice, parsley and orzo, over low heat for at least 6–8 hours.
3. Remove the bay leaves about 30 minutes before serving. Shred the chicken with 2 forks and add the lemon juice, parsley, orzo, salt and pepper. I advise you to stir every 10 minutes, or the orzo will stick to the bottom of the slow cooker. Serve immediately and enjoy!

Nutrition

Calories:	253.7	**Carbohydrates:**	44.1 g	**Protein:**	17.1 g
Fat:	1.6 g	**Fiber:**	2.6 g		

FRIED RICE

Full of Vegetables

In this delicious recipe, you will learn how to make a simple and satisfying fried rice with vegetables – perfect for dinner! This vegetarian recipe contains vegetables and brown rice. The recipe produces 2 to 3 moderate servings.

INGREDIENTS

2	Tbsp.	Avocado oil or saffron oil, divided
2		Eggs, beaten together
1	Medium	Red pepper
2	Medium	Carrots, chopped (about ½ cup)
2	Cups	Additional vegetables, cut into very small pieces for quick cooking (see photos for size reference; options include snow peas, asparagus, broccoli, cabbage, peppers and/or peas fresh or frozen – do not defrost first)
¼	Tsp.	Salt, to taste
1	Tbsp.	Fresh ground ginger
	Pinch	Red pepper flakes
2	Cups	Cooked brown rice
1	Cup	Green vegetables (optional) such as spinach, kale or tatsoi
3		Green onions, finely chopped
1	Tbsp.	Tamari or soy sauce with low sodium **
1	Tsp.	Toasted sesame oil
		Garlic or sriracha chili sauce, to serve (optional)

INSTRUCTIONS

1. Over medium heat, heat a large or medium stainless steel pan until a few drops of water sprinkled in the pan evaporate. Add ½ teaspoon of oil and tilt the pan to cover the bottom. Add the eggs and scramble, swirling the pan so that it coats or covers the bottom. Cook until slightly set, turning or stirring as needed. Put the eggs into a bowl and scrape the pan with a heat-resistant spatula.

2. Restore the pan back onto medium heat and add a tablespoon of oil. For the next 3 to 5 minutes, sauté the onions and carrots. Cook, stirring often, until the onions become semi opaque and the carrots softened.

3. Add the rest of the vegetables and salt. Continue to cook, stirring occasionally (do not stir too often or the vegetables will not be able to turn golden along the edges), until the vegetables turn golden brown in color, about 3 to 5 minutes. Meanwhile, using the edge of a spatula or spoon, break the scrambled eggs into small pieces.

4. Using a large spatula or spoon, transfer the contents of the pan to a bowl with the cooked eggs. Add the remaining 1 tablespoon of oil into the pan and heat. Add the ginger, garlic and red pepper flakes and cook until they are fragrant, stirring occasionally, for about 30 seconds. Add the rice and mix well to combine. Cook, stirring at intervals, until the rice is golden along the edges, about 3 to 5 minutes.

5. Add the green onions, then stir to combine. Add the cooked vegetables and eggs, stir to combine. Remove the pan from the heat and stir in the oil (both tamari and sesame). Taste, and add a little more tamari if you'd like more soy but be very careful not to overdo it or it will stifle the other flavors!

6. Divide into bowls and serve immediately. You're free to serve with sriracha or chili garlic sauce.

Nutrition

Calories:	400	Carbohydrate:	54.4 g	Protein:	11.5 g
Fat:	16.9 g	Fiber:	11.6 g		

LOADED CHICKEN SOUP

with beans

This delicious recipe is a mixture of winter vegetables, tomatoes, parmesan, herbs, pasta and beans, all cooked in one pan to create a bowl of healthy, hot soup!

INGREDIENTS

3	Thick sliced	Bacon slices, chopped (optional)
¼	Cup	Extra-virgin olive oil
1	Medium	Yellow onion, finely chopped
4		Carrots, finely chopped
2		Celery stalks, finely chopped
6	Cloves	Garlic, chopped or grated
		Kosher salt and black pepper
3–4	Cup	Chicken or vegetable broth low sodium
		Tomatoes, diced, 1 can (14 ounces)
1	Large	Green cabbage, chopped.
1		Parmesan rind, plus grated parmesan, for serving
2		Bay leaves
3	Sprigs	Fresh thyme
1	Sprig	Fresh rosemary
1	Pinch	Crushed red pepper flakes
1	Oz.	Short pasta
		Cannella beans (12 oz), drained and washed

INSTRUCTIONS

1. Begin by setting Instant Pot to the sauté mode. Add the bacon and cook until crispy, at least 5 minutes.

2. Add olive oil, onion, carrot, celery, garlic and a pinch of salt and pepper to Instant Pot. Cook 8 to 10 minutes until the vegetables are cooked through. Turn off the Instant Pot.

3. To 3 cups broth, add the tomato, cabbage, Grated parmesan, bay leaf, thyme and rosemary. Season with salt, pepper and chopped red pepper flakes. Cover and cook at high pressure for about 10 minutes.

4. Next, bring a large pot of salted water to a boil. Cook pasta according to package Instructions, until al dente. Drain immediately.

5. After cooking,. Take out the parmesan rind, bay leaf, thyme, rosemary and discard. Add the beans and half of the pasta. Add more pasta as desired. If you like, you can add remaining onion until desired constancy.

6. Divide the soup between the bowls and sprinkle with parmesan. Enjoy!

Nutrition

Calories:	306	**Carbohydrates:**	24 g	**Protein:**	16 g
Fiber:	2 g				

ITALIAN RAVIOLI

with spinach, artichokes, capers, and tomatoes

In this recipe, the vegetables are sautéed in olive oil – a recipe for meatless pasta, Mediterranean style that needs no meat at all. This dish will definitely fill you up!

INGREDIENTS

8	Oz.	Ravioli (cheese ravioli or pesto ravioli)
2	Tbsp.	Olive oil
⅓	Cup	Chopped sun-dried tomatoes
¾	Cup	Minced artichoke hearts
3	Tbsp.	Capers, drained
½	Tsp.	Italian spices (seasoning)
2	Cups	Fresh spinach
1	Tbsp.	Olive oil and more (optional)
⅓	Cup	Parmesan, chopped

INSTRUCTIONS

1. Begin by cooking the ravioli until al dente. Drain immediately.

2. Over medium heat in a skillet pan, heat 2 tablespoons of olive oil. Transfer the chopped sun-dried tomatoes, artichokes, capers, the Italian seasoning and cook for 2 minutes. Introduce the fresh spinach and continue cooking and stir until the spinach is about a quarter of the size it was before being cooked.

3. To the pan containing sautéed vegetables, over medium heat, add the cooked ravioli and 1 tablespoon olive oil and stir. The dish should be sufficiently salted with capers. Otherwise, add more salt (or capers) if necessary.

4. Sprinkle with chopped parmesan cheese before serving.

Nutrition

Calories:	384	**Carbohydrates:**	30 g	**Protein:**	12 g
Fat:	23 g	**Fiber:**	4 g		

SAGANAKI PRAWN
Stew

Always wanted to visit Greece? We will bring a little taste to you! This is the perfect comfort stew for those movie nights! Its quick and has a real burst of flavor!

INGREDIENTS

¼	Cup	Olive oil
1	Cup	Fresh Prawns
1		Red onion, finely chopped
2		Garlic cloves, finely crushed
1	Large	Red pepper, finely chopped
1		Bell pepper, any variety, finely chopped
3	Tbsp.	Ouzo
7	Ounces	Tomatoes or 2 large tomatoes, puréed in a blender
¼	Cup	Flat parsley, finely chopped
3.5	Ounces	Feta
		Salt and pepper for spice

INSTRUCTIONS

1. Over medium-high heat, in a large deep frying skillet, heat the olive oil. After heating, add the onion, garlic and chili. Let the mixture soften and become transparent.

2. Add the prawns and sauté for a few minutes.

3. Add the ouzo, tomato, parsley, salt and pepper and bring to a boil. When you reach the boiling point, reduce the temperature to medium-low. Cook for about 10 minutes.

4. Transfer the prawn mixture to oven-safe ceramic bowls and add the feta cheese on top. Put in a roasting pan and place under a hot grill until the feta cheese melts and seeps into the sauce.

5. Remove from oven, garnish with parsley and serve.

Nutrition

Calories:	303	**Carbohydrates:**	7 g	**Protein:**	18 g
Fat:	20 g				

GREEK RICE SPINACH

(Spanakoryzo)

Delicious low-budget meal or recipe ready in a few minutes! This simple, tasty and authentic Greek spinach rice makes a vegetarian meal. Fresh dill, garlic cloves and lemon juice give it exceptional flavor and aroma.

INGREDIENTS

21	Oz.	Fresh or frozen spinach
⅓	Cup	Olive oil
⅓		Small red onion, finely chopped
2		Chives, finely chopped
2	Medium	Garlic cloves, minced
3.5	Oz.	Long grain rice
2	Oz.	Short grain rice
1	Tbsp.	Chopped fresh dill
½		Lemon, juiced
		Salt and pepper

INSTRUCTIONS

1. Over medium heat, in a large–size cooking pot, heat ½ of the olive oil.
2. Next, cook the onion and garlic until golden. Add spinach and cook 2 to 3 minutes, stirring with a wooden spoon until drained and softened. Add 3 cups of water and reduce the heat to medium. Simmer while covered for at least 20 minutes.
3. Add the short grain rice and simmer for another 10 minutes. Season with salt and pepper and add the dill and remaining olive oil, together with the long grain rice. Ensure there is sufficient water in the pot for the rice to cook, then cover and simmer for another 20–30 minutes or until the rice is fully cooked.
4. Add the fresh lemon juice. Turn off the heat and serve immediately. While serving, you can add a few extra drops of lemon juice, depending on your preference.

Note: If you are using fresh spinach, you can also use stalks too. Be sure to wash and remove any dirt, then slice the bottom crosswise for easier cooking.

Nutrition

Calories:	740	**Carbohydrates:**	82 g	**Protein:**	15 g
Fat:	42 g	**Fiber:**	10 g		

BAKED HALIBUT
with Vegetables

This delicious recipe requires very little time – you can make baked halibut every night of the week. The secret to its incredible flavor lies in the sauce!

Serves:

INGREDIENTS

For the sauce:

2		Lemons
		Juice of 2 lemons
1	Cup	Extra-virgin olive oil
2	Tbsp.	Freshly ground garlic
4		Sprigs rosemerry
1	Tsp.	Salt, more for later
½	Tbsp.	Ground black pepper
1	Tsp.	Dried oregano
¾	Tsp.	Ground coriander

For Fish:

1	Lb.	Green beans
1	Lb.	Cherry tomatoes
1	Large	Yellow onion, sliced
2.25	Lbs.	Halibut fillet, cut into ½ pieces

INSTRUCTIONS

1. Preheat the oven to 425° F.

2. In a medium-size bowl, combine the sauce ingredients. Add the green beans, tomatoes, onions and stir, then garnish with the sauce. Using a spatula, move the vegetables to a clean baking sheet. Using a spatula, move the vegetables to a clean baking sheet, making sure they are spread in a single layer.

3. Next, add the halibut fillet strips to the remaining sauce; stir to coat. Position the fillet on the baking sheet next to the vegetables and pour the rest of the sauce over the top.

4. Sprinkle the halibut and vegetables with more salt and pepper.

5. Bake in the preheated oven at 425° F for 15 minutes. Place the baking sheet on the upper rack of the oven and bake for another 3 minutes, watching carefully. The cherry tomatoes should begin popping under the broiler!

6. When done, remove the baked halibut and the vegetables from the oven. You are free to serve with any grain or pasta.

Nutrition

Calories:	390	Carbohydrates:	8.8 g	Protein:	17.5 g
Fat:	31.3 g				

MEDITERRANEAN CAULIFLOWER

Rice Skillet

This recipe tastes incredibly good and is very suitable for any meal of the day. It's a gluten free, Paleo and Whole30 recipe!

INGREDIENTS

2	Tbsp.	Olive oil
½	Medium	Onion, diced
1	Cup	(about 4 oz.) Sliced mushrooms
1	Medium	Garlic clove, minced
10-12	Oz.	Cauliflower rice *(see notes for making your own or using frozen)*
1	Small	Zucchini, cut in half lengthwise and sliced
1	Cup	Broccoli florets
⅓ – ½	Cup	Vegetable broth
2	Cups	Spinach, cut into large pieces
3–4	Tbsp.	Sun-dried tomatoes (bottled in olive oil)
		Salt to taste
		Paprika to taste

INSTRUCTIONS

1. Add oil to the skillet and heat over medium or slightly high heat.

2. Add in the onion and sliced mushrooms. Sauté about 5–6 minutes, or until the onion turns opaque and the mushrooms begin to brown. (Most of the liquid should have evaporated.)

3. Add the garlic and cook for another minute.

4. Next, add the cauliflower rice, and broccoli florets. Add ⅓ cup of broth.

5. Further cook over low heat to evaporate the broth and cook the vegetables for another 5–6 minutes. If necessary, add a little more broth to the skillet pan to continue cooking. (At this point, you should only have about 1 to 2 tablespoons of liquid at the bottom of the pan.)

6. Next, add the spinach and sun-dried tomatoes and cook for about 3–4 minutes to thicken the spinach.

7. Season with salt and pepper to taste, top with your favorite protein if desired.

Nutrition

Calories:	119	**Carbohydrates:**	8.7 g	**Protein:**	3.9 g
Fat:	8 g	**Fiber:**	3.4 g		

SIMPLE MEDITERRANEAN PASTA

Made with Olive Oil

One of my favorite Mediterranean delicacies – pasta with olive oil! Perfect dish for dinner to enjoy with friends and family.

INGREDIENTS

1	Lb.	Thin spaghetti
½	Cup	Extra-virgin olive oil
3		Garlic cloves, crushed
		Salt to taste
1	Cup	Chopped fresh parsley
½	Oz.	Tomatoes, cut in half
3		Green onions, chopped into ¼ inch
1	Tbsp.	Black pepper
1 ¼	Cup	Pressed artichoke hearts (optional)
¼	Cup	Olives, pitted and halved (optional)
¼	Cup	Crushed feta cheese, more if desired
10		Fresh basil leaves, grated
1	Zest	Lemon
		Crushed red pepper flakes, optional

INSTRUCTIONS

1. Follow the package directions to cook the thin spaghetti until al dente (it can take up to 6 minutes to cook in hot boiling water with salt and olive oil).

2. Watch over the pasta until it's almost done. Add olive oil to a medium skillet and gently apply heat, add the garlic and a pinch of salt. Cook for 10 seconds, stirring regularly. Add the parsley, tomato and chopped nuts. Simmer until heated through, about 30 seconds.

3. Once the pasta is cooked, remove from the heat, drain the cooking water and return to the pot. Pour the hot olive oil sauce over the pasta and stir to coat. Add the black pepper and toss to cover.

4. Add the rest of the ingredients and stir occasionally. Serve in pasta bowls and garnish each with several basil leaves and feta cheese if desired.

Nutrition

Calories:	461.7	**Carbohydrates:**	65.8 g	**Protein:**	11.4 g
Fat:	13.5 g	**Fiber:**	3.9 g		

SAUSAGE WITH BRAISED CABBAGE

This delicious and hearty sausage recipe will brighten up your dinner – naturally low in carbs, gluten free and Paleo!

INGREDIENTS

2	Tbsp.	Olive oil
1	Tsp.	Worcestershire sauce
1		Medium green cabbage
1		Red pepper, cut into large pieces
1	Medium	Onion, chopped
2		Carrots, chopped
2		Garlic cloves, minced
		Salt to taste
2	Tbsp.	Paprika (optional)
1	Cup	Water
6–8		Sausages: you can use any sausage of your choice

INSTRUCTIONS

1. Set your oven and preheat to a temperature of 350 F°.

2. In a large oven-proof skillet, heat 1 tablespoon olive oil. Cook the sausages for a few minutes on each side until golden. Put the cooked sausage on a plate.

3. Add 1 more tablespoon of olive oil to the pan and heat over medium heat. Add vegetables and cook covered for about 5 to 7 minutes until softened, stirring occasionally.

4. Place the sausage and 1 cup of water in the skillet, mix everything and place in a preheated oven. Cook covered with aluminum foil for about 25 minutes. Take off the foil and cook for another 5 minutes. Serve hot.

Nutrition

Calories:	496	**Carbohydrates:**	23 g	**Protein:**	29 g
Fat:	37 g	**Fiber:**	7 g		

SOUR CREAM
and Berries Brûlée

Dessert has never been much easier than this. Just three ingredients, berries, sour cream and brown sugar, are combined to create a juicy, creamy, crunchy and caramelized sweetness. It sounds special and imaginative, but it is quite easy to assemble, making it the perfect choice for all your dessert needs at a summer party.

INGREDIENTS

2	Cups	Fresh raspberries
2	Cups	Fresh strawberries, sliced
2	Cups	Sour cream
½	Cup	Dark or light brown sugar

INSTRUCTIONS

1. Place the rack in the upper third of the oven (6 to 8 inches away from the element) and heat the broiler to a high level. Arrange the strawberries and raspberries evenly on a baking sheet.

2. Cover the top with sour cream. Using a spatula, gently spread out the berries. Spread the brown sugar over the sour cream using your hands.

3. Bake in the oven for about 5 minutes until the sugar has melted and just begins to caramelize. Take care during this process because the sugar can rapidly go from being caramelized to burnt. Serve immediately.

Nutrition

Calories:	172	**Carbohydrates:** 17.1 g	**Protein:**	1.8 g
Fat:	11.5 g	**Fiber:** 2.8 g		

WHIPPED YOGURT
with Nuts and Apples

You can top off your whipped yogurt with anything tasty. I've chosen cinnamon apples because they seem perfect for the season. However, this recipe is fully customizable, so if you prefer to use any other fruits, you have absolute freedom!

INGREDIENTS

½	Cup	Heavy cream
1	Cup	Plain Greek yogurt
2	Tbsp.	Unsalted butter
1	Tbsp.	Honey
2	Tbsp.	Sugar
2		Semi-hard apples, cut into 1/2-inch cubes
¼	Cup	Walnuts, toasted and chopped into rough pieces
¼	Tsp.	Ground cinnamon

INSTRUCTIONS

1. In a medium-size bowl, combine cream, yogurt and honey. Using a hand mixer, generously beat the mixture until fully thickened.

2. In a large skillet, heat the butter over medium heat. Add the apples and 1 tablespoon of sugar to the pan.

3. Mix well and cook the apples for 6 to 8 minutes, stirring occasionally to prevent sticking. Monitor until well softened. As soon as it's softened, sprinkle the apples with the rest of the cinnamon and sugar and cook for another 2 to 3 minutes. Take off the heat and let stand for about 5 minutes to cool.

4. For serving, add a generous portion of whipped cream to each bowl. You are free to top with toasted nuts and slightly warm apples.

Nutrition

Calories:	315	Carbohydrates:	26.7 g	Protein:	6.4 g
Fat:	21.9 g	Fiber:	2.4 g		

HOW TO MAKE GRANITA
from Any Fruit

Have you ever craved awesome frozen treats? Then look no further. Here, I'll introduce you to granita. This recipe is an iced fruit dessert produced using fresh fruit and water. It's mixed and frozen until icy then crumbled with a fork and refrozen once more!

The result is an awesome, crunchy fruit ice cream that can be eaten alone. You are free to serve with anything from yogurt to cocktails.

INGREDIENTS

¼	Cup	Freshly squeezed lime juice (2 limes)
4	Cups	Fruit, such as seedless watermelon, strawberry or peach (about 1 pound)
⅓	Cup	Granulated sugar
		Yogurt, to serve (optional)
⅛	Tsp.	Kosher salt
¼	Cup	Granulated sugar

For the lime zest topping (optional):

½	Tsp.	Red pepper flakes
1	Tbsp.	Finely grated lime zest (1 lime)

INSTRUCTIONS

1. Combine lime juice, fruit, sugar and salt in a blender or food processor equipped with a juicing blade. Purée until smooth, about 1 minute.

2. Pour the purée into a 9x13-inch metal pan. The purée should be about ½ inch deep. However, it is okay if the pan is deeper; it just takes longer to freeze. Freeze for 30 minutes.

3. Remove the pan from the freezer after 30 minutes. The puree should start to freeze, especially around the top and edges. Scrape the mixture with a fork and return to the freezer. Repeat this procedure every 30 minutes for a total of 4 hours. Granita is made when the mixture is completely frozen and has a bumpy rough, dry, texture.

4. Use topping (optional). In a small bowl, combine the sugar, lemon zest and peppers. Reserve until ready to serve.

5. Pour into bowls and serve – pour the granita in bowls alone or with yogurt. You are free to top with lime zest as well!

Nutrition

Calories:	153	**Carbohydrates:** 39.5 g		**Protein:**	1.2 g
Fat:	0.3 g	**Fiber:**	1.0 g		

FRUIT SALAD
with Lemon Syrup and Vanilla

I suppose one could argue that dressing a fruit salad is somewhat like gilding the lily, especially when the fruit is at the height of the season. In that regard, I say a little extra sparkle never hurt anybody!

INGREDIENTS

For the syrup:

1		Vanilla pod
3	Medium	Lemons, washed and dried
¼	Cup	Water
½	Cup	Granulated sugar

For the fruit salad:

2	Cups	Cherries, pitted and cut in half
1	Cup	Thinly sliced rhubarb (1 large stem)
2	Medium	Peaches, diced and sliced ¼-inch thick
1	Generous cup	Raspberries
2.25	Pounds	Strawberries, peeled and sliced

Optional Ingredients:

	Bee pollen
	Fresh mint
	Black sesame seeds
	Roasted coconut flakes
	Whipped cream

INSTRUCTIONS

Make a syrup:

1. Using the vegetable peeler, peel the zest from one lemon. Juice the lemon until you have ¼ cup of lemon juice, then set aside. Use a sharp knife to cut the vanilla bean lengthwise. Scrape the vanilla bean seeds from the pod using the tip of the knife. In a medium-size pan, add the seeds, pod, lemon zest, sugar.

Prepare a fruit salad:

4. In a large bowl, add the extracted vanilla from the pod and mix in the lemon juice, mix well. Let it stand at room temperature for 15 minutes.

5. Gently mix the cherries, peaches and strawberries, adding more syrup if necessary.

2. Cook over medium heat, stirring occasionally, until the sugar completely dissolves. Take the pan off the heat and add the lemon juice you had set aside. Let it cool to room temperature, and then remove the lemon zest and vanilla pod.

3. Preserve the syrup in the refrigerator (in an airtight container) until ready for use.

Transfer to the serving dish and sprinkle the raspberries over the top. Serve immediately.

6. You can add extra whipped cream and syrup or any side toppings.

Nutrition

Calories:	235	**Carbohydrates:**	58.7 g	**Protein:**	3.0 g
Fat:	1.0 g	**Fiber:**	8.1 g		

FRUIT GALETTE

Galette is a French dough similar to a pie or pastry; it's a mass of dough wrapped around a filling of fruit, butter and sugar. No special cake pan is needed for this pie or pastry, just a nice, flat baking surface.

INGREDIENTS - *For dough:*

1 ½	Cups	All purpose-flour
½	Tsp.	Salt
¼	Cup	Finely ground white corn flour
1	Tbsp.	Granulated sugar
¼	Cup	Ice water
8	Tbsp.	Unsalted cold butter, diced

Fruit Filling

½ to 1	Lb.	Stone fruit (plumps or peaches), cut in half, pitted and sliced ¼ to 1-inch thick
1	Tbsp.	All-purpose flour
⅓	Cup	Turbinado sugar, plus more to sprinkle
½	Tsp.	Freshly grated nutmeg
½	Tbsp.	Ground cinnamon
1	Tbsp.	Unsalted butter, diced
¼	Tsp.	Salt
1	Tbsp.	Water
1	Large	Egg
1	Tbsp.	Light-colored jam (such as peach, apple or mango chutney)

INSTRUCTIONS

1. **Make galette dough**: In a food processor fitted with the blade attachment, pulse the flour, cornmeal, sugar and salt together until well mixed. Include the butter and pulse until it starts to come together at least 7 to 10 pulses. If there are a few big pieces of butter left, it is fine. Sprinkle in 2 tablespoons of ice water and pulse until the dough is crumbly textured but holds together when compressed, around 4 pulses. If the mix is dry, pulse in about 2 tablespoon of ice water, 1 tablespoon at a time.

2. Cool the dough and roll into a piece of plastic wrap. Wrap it completely and refrigerate for 1 hour.

3. **Preheat the oven**: Set the rack in the middle of the oven and preheat to 400° F.

4. **Roll the dough:** Roll out the dough and place it on a piece of parchment paper. Cover with another piece of parchment. Roll the dough into a 12-inch-thick round about $^1/_8$ of an inch. Fold the parchment and dough on a baking sheet and remove the top layer of parchment.

5. **Make a fruit garnish:** Combine the sliced fruit, flour, ¼ cup turbinado sugar, nutmeg, cinnamon and salt In a large bowl.

6. **Arrange the galette:** Place the fruit filling on the dough, dip it slightly in the middle and leave a 2-inch border around the edge. Fold the dough ring up on the edge of the filling. Sparsely distribute the butter cubes on the fruit. Beat the egg with 1 tablespoon of water. Mix the crust with the egg and sprinkle with more turbinado sugar.

7. **Bake**: Bake in the oven until it turns golden brown and the fruit becomes cooked, approximately 30 to 35 minutes. Transfer the parchment with the galette to a wire rack and allow to completely cool.

8. Cover the fruit with glaze and serve with the galette. Dilute the jam with 1 teaspoon of water. Cut the galette into quarters and serve immediately.

Nutrition

Calories:	286	Carbohydrates:	36.9 g	Protein:	4.0 g
Fat:	14.0 g	Fiber:	1.6 g		

STRAWBERRIES
in Red Wine

Fresh, in-season strawberries do not require much to dress them up – they can just be enjoyed on their own. Yet if you would like to turn them into a dessert deserving of a party dinner, you would not have to try too much harder. Just let these berries swim for a little bit in a blend of red wine, natural sugar and vanilla, and they are turned into something much greater than you could ever imagine.

INGREDIENTS

1	Lb.	Strawberries, halved, or quartered if very large (about 3 cups)
2	Cups	Fruity dry red wine, such as zinfandel or merlot
⅓	Cup	Packed brown sugar
2	Tsp.	Vanilla extract
		Crème fraîche or whipped cream, for serving if desired

INSTRUCTIONS

1. Transfer the strawberries into a large bowl and sprinkle with brown sugar. Add the red wine, vanilla and mix to combine. Cover and refrigerate at least 2 hrs.

2. Next, add the strawberries into a medium size or small bowl containing a little water and serve with a large drop of crème fraîche or whipped cream.

Nutrition

Calories:	198	**Carbohydrates:**	25.8 g	**Protein:**	0.9 g
Fat:	0.3 g	**Fiber:**	2.3 g		

BRÛLÉED FRUIT
with Mascarpone Yogurt Sauce

I'm always looking for ways to enjoy a fruit dessert. Taking a page from a French classic, this recipe is a crème brûlée dessert, with pieces of juicy fruit sprinkled with brown sugar, broiled until caramelized on top, and then topped with a creamy mascarpone yogurt and macadamia nuts.

INGREDIENTS

For fruit:

1	Tsp.	Vanilla extract
¼	Cup	Packed brown sugar
¼	Tsp.	Fine salt
4		Strawberries
2		Blood oranges or navel oranges
½		Pineapple
1	Large	Mango

To finish(Topping):

⅓	Cup	Mascarpone cheese
1	Cup	Plain Greek yogurt
½	Cup	Toasted macadamia nuts, coarsely chopped

INSTRUCTIONS

1. Place the oven rack 6 inches from the broiler and heat. Put the vanilla, brown sugar and salt in a large bowl.

2. Cut the top off the strawberries and slice lengthwise.

3. Cut the orange crosswise into a ½-inch thick disk and add to the bowl with the brown sugar mixture.

4. Peel a mango, cut the fleshy part away from the pit and cut the fruit into ¼-inch thick slices; add to the bowl of citrus. Cut the pineapple peel, cut away the core, then cut the fruit into long strips ¼-inch thick; add to the bowl of citrus.

5. Lightly coat the fruit with the brown sugar with your hands. You will notice a dissolu-tion of the brown sugar and the juice will be released from the fruit. With your hands, lift the fruit from the juice onto a rimmed baking sheet; distribute well. Set aside the bowl and juices.

6. Broil for about 10 minutes until golden brown (watch keenly and turn the pan if necessary). Remove the pan and place on a wire rack to cool gradually.

7. **For topping:** Use 3 tablespoons of the juice from the bowl. Add yogurt and mascarpone. Whisk gently until smooth throughout.

8. Break apart your favorite cookie, place in the bottom of a deep cup and pour the mixture over top, garnish with strawberries, mint and macadamia nuts.

Nutrition

Calories:	304	**Carbohydrates:**	41.3 g	**Protein:**	6.6 g
Fat:	14.7 g	**Fiber:**	4.5 g		

FRENCH CHOCOLATE
and Clafoutis Pear

The French are known for their outstanding attitude towards breakfast. This chocolate recipe can be the perfect way to start your day!

INGREDIENTS

1	Cup	Whole milk
1	Tbsp.	Unsalted butter
3	Large	Eggs
½	Cup	Granulated sugar
⅓	Cup	All-purpose flour
1	Tsp.	Vanilla extract
¼	Tsp.	Fine salt
1	Pound	Large ripe pears (*like comice or d'anjou, about two large*), peeled, cored and sliced
2	Tbsp.	Unsweetened natural cocoa powder
½	Cup	Cherries (*optional*)
3	Ounces	Dark chocolate, cut into large pieces

INSTRUCTIONS

1. Place the rack in the middle of the oven and preheat to 400° F. Use the butter to coat a 10-inch cast iron skillet. Keep aside.

2. Add the sugar, milk, vanilla and eggs into a blender or food processor. Let blend for about 20 seconds, until the batter is quite smooth. Add the flour, powder, cocoa and salt, and mix well.

3. In a prepared pan, arrange the pear slices in a layer, in a circle. Spread the batter evenly over the pears, and then sprinkle the chopped chocolate all over.

4. Bake until the clafoutis is puffy, firm and lightly browned around the edges, about 35 minutes. Place the pan on a wire rack and let cool for 15 minutes.

5. Divide nicely into wedges and serve!

Nutrition

Calories:	214	**Carbohydrates:**	34.5 g	**Protein:**	4.8 g
Fat:	7.8 g	**Fiber:**	3.0 g		

FRUIT CRUMBLES
with Any Type of Fruit

Crumble is a simple wild fruit recipe that contains a crisp, rich coating that turns any fruit into a dazzling dessert. It is excellent for summer lunches and barbecue terraces. Making a crumble is so simple that you hardly require a recipe to make it.

Once you know the basics of making breadcrumb toppings and how to make a fruit topping, you can choose any fruit or combination of fruits from any season. Here are three basic steps you need to know in other to make classic fruit crumbles.

INGREDIENTS

The fillings:

1	Cup	Granulated sugar, depending on the sweetness of the fruit
7	Cups	Fruit, enough to almost fill the pan
2	Tsp.	Freshly squeezed lemon juice
1 to 3	Tbsp.	Cornstarch, depending on the juiciness of the fruit
1	Tsp.	Ground spices, such as cinnamon, ginger or nutmeg (optional)

Crumble toppings:

1	Cup	Multipurpose flour or oats
½	Cup	Light or dark brown sugar
½	Tsp.	Ground cinnamon (optional)
1	Tsp.	Baking powder
8	Tbsp.	Unsalted butter, at room temperature
½	Tsp.	Salt

INSTRUCTIONS

1. Place the rack in the middle of the oven and preheat to 375° F. Gently coat a baking dish with butter and set aside.

2. Fruit filling: If necessary, cut the fruit into cubes, removing the stems, seeds or inedible parts. In a large bowl, combine the fruit with the lemon juice, sugar, spices and cornstarch.

Add more sugar and slightly less lemon juice when cooking with tart fruits, like blackberries, rhubarb, and less sugar, but more lemon juice for sweet fruits, like plums and peaches.

You can use more cornstarch with very juicy fruits like plums and less with firm fruits like apples. However, do not worry: whatever the proportion of these ingredients, your crumble will be certainly be delicious.

3. Add the fruit filling into the baking dish and the fruit filling as well.

4. Prepare the crumble toppings: Combine or whisk the sugar, flour, baking powder, cinnamon and salt in a large bowl. Slice the butter into several large pieces and mix well into the dry ingredients. Mix the butter with the dry ingredients until large heavy crumbs form.

5. Sprinkle the crumble over the fruit.

6. Next, bake the crumble. Bake well for about 30 to 35 minutes until the fruit juices make bubbles around the edges of the pan.

7. Let the crumble cool for at least 15 minutes before serving.

Nutrition

Calories:	349	**Carbohydrates:** 51.8 g		**Protein:**	3.4 g
Fat:	15.8 g	**Fiber:**	3.6 g		

GLOSSARY OF COOKING TERMS

BEAT: To stir rapidly to make a mixture smooth, using a whisk, spoon, or mixer.

CUT IN: To distribute a solid fat in flour using a cutting motion, with 2 knives used scissors-fashion or using a pastry blender, until divided evenly into tiny pieces. Usually refers to making pastry.

DEEP-FRY: To cook by completely immersing food in hot fat.

DRIZZLE: To pour melted butter, oil, syrup, melted chocolate, or other liquid back and forth over food in a fine stream.

GARNISH: To decorate a dish both to enhance its appearance and to provide a flavorful foil. Parsley, lemon slices, raw vegetables, chopped chives, and other herbs are all forms of garnishes.

GLAZE: To coat foods with glossy mixtures such as jellies or sauces.

GRATE: To rub foods against a serrated surface to produce shredded or fine bits.

GRILL: Grilling food is applying dry heat to food either from above or below. In South Africa, grilling refers to cooking food under the grill in your oven (in the States this is called broiling) or can also refer to cooking food in a pan with grill lines.

MINCE: To cut into tiny pieces, usually with a knife.

PARBOIL: To partially cook by boiling. Usually done to prepare food for final cooking by another method.

PURÉE: To blend in a blender or process in a food processor or food mill until food is smooth and lump-free. The term also refers to the food that has been puréed.

ROAST: To cook a large piece of meat or poultry uncovered with dry heat in an oven.

SAUTÉ: To cook gently in a little fat, stirring and shaking the ingredients for much of the cooking time. In French, the term translates "to jump."

SEAR: To brown the surface of meat by quick-cooking over high heat in order to seal in the meat's juices.

SIMMER: To cook in liquid just below the boiling point; bubbles form but do not burst on the surface of the liquid.

SKIM: To remove surface foam or fat from a liquid.

STEW: To cook covered over low heat in a liquid.

STIR-FRY: To quickly cook small pieces of food over high heat, stirring constantly.

WHIP: To beat food with a whisk or mixer to incorporate air and produce volume.

WHISK: To beat ingredients (such as heavy or whipping cream, eggs, salad dressings, or sauces) with a fork or whisk to mix, blend, or incorporate air.

ZEST: The outer, colored part of the peel of citrus fruit.

CONCLUSION

Thank you so much for securing a copy of the Mediterranean Refresh Cookbook. We believe you have acquired enough recipe ideas for a wide variety of delicious Mediterranean Cuisines!

Eat Healthy, Stay Healthy! Good Food CHANGES the Mood!

© **Peapil Publishing**